INTERNATIONAL SOCIALISM ★

A quarterly journal of socialist theory

Spring 1999
Contents

D0550649

Editorial

Issue 82 of INTERNATIONAL SOCIALISM, quarterly journal of the Socialist Workers Party (Britain)

Published March 1999
Copyright © International Socialism
Distribution/subscriptions: International Socialism,
PO Box 82, London E3
American distribution: B de Boer, 113 East Center St, Nutley,
New Jersey 07110
Subscriptions and back copies: PO Box 16085, Chicago
Illinois 60616
Editorial and production: 0171 538 5821
Sales and subscriptions: 0171 538 5821
American sales: 773 665 7337

ISBN 1 898876 44 4

Printed by BPC Wheatons Ltd, Exeter, England
Typeset by East End Offset, London E3
Cover by Sherborne Design Ltd

For details of back copies see the end pages of this book

Subscription rates for one year (four issues) are:

Britain and overseas (surface):	individual	£14 ($30)
	institutional	£25
Air speeded supplement:	North America	£3
	Europe/South America	£3
	elsewhere	£4

Note to contributors

The deadline for articles intended for issue 84 of *International Socialism* is 1 July 1999

All contributions should be double spaced with wide margins. Please submit two copies. If you write your contribution using a computer, please also supply a disk, together with details of the computer and programme used.

INTERNATIONAL SOCIALISM ★

A quarterly journal of socialist theory

THE UNRAVELLING of Tony Blair's government has accelerated since he lost his key adviser Peter Mandelson in a sleaze scandal late last year. Since then the crisis in the Labour Party in Wales and in Scotland, followed by the news that Ken Livingstone will challenge Blairite attempts to exclude him as the Labour candidate for London mayor, have made it clear that the deep dissatisfaction with New Labour is finding expression within the party itself. And all this comes before the worst of the recession hits the British economy and before the government faces widespread industrial struggle. Lindsey German charts the decline in Blair's fortunes and outlines a socialist alternative to New Labour.

ECONOMIC TURMOIL is still spreading across the globe more than a year after it first hit South East Asia. In our last issue we examined this crisis in detail. Here *The Guardian*'s economic analysts Dan Atkinson and Larry Elliott use the account of the world economy first developed in their book *The Age of Insecurity* to present a Keynesian perspective on some aspects of the crisis. A new collection of essays by another new Keynesian, *The Observer* editor Will Hutton, is reviewed by Peter Morgan. Rob Hoveman brings this issue's continuing coverage of key debates in economics to a close with his review of a recently published account of the changes in post-war capitalism by Marxist writer Robert Brenner.

JOHN MOLYNEUX'S defence of modern art in *International Socialism* 80 has proved controversial and here we publish a critical response by Chris Nineham. Our book reviews are Paul McGarr's examination of Jim Wolfreys and Pete Fysh's *The Politics of Racism in France* and Brian Manning's appreciation of Norah Carlin's new account of the causes of the English Revolution.

SCOTLAND'S INDEPENDENCE has always had a fierce left wing champion in Tom Nairn, whose work has done much to shape socialist thinking on the future of the British state. Neil Davidson's detailed examination of Nairn's work, the latest in our 'In perspective' series, carefully exposes the weaknesses in his position and suggests a more theoretically consistent alternative.

Editor: John Rees. Assistant editors: Alex Callinicos, Chris Harman, John Molyneux, Lindsey German, Colin Sparks, Mike Gonzalez, Peter Morgan, Mike Haynes, Judy Cox, Megan Trudell, Mark O'Brien, Rob Hoveman and Michael Lavalette.

The Blair project cracks

LINDSEY GERMAN

Whatever Labour supporters thought they were voting for on 1 May 1997, they believed they were rejecting Tory policies. They wanted no more privatisation, better public services, greater job security. They wanted an end to the influence of sleazy businessmen, a halt to the MPs who listened to professional lobbyists rather than their constituents, and a greater say in decision making. They wanted to stop the vested interests, from country landowners to giant supermarkets, dictating what working people should do. Nearly half way through the term of a landslide Labour government, none of these wishes has been achieved. Tony Blair's Labour government is noted more for its conservatism than its radicalism. All those who most identified with Labour's aspirations—for greater equality and fairness, for a curbing of the bosses' worst excesses, for ending the worst poverty in generations—now find themselves disappointed at the lack of change. Those traditionally most hostile to Labour—big business, the press, the champions of free enterprise—are pleasantly surprised that their wealth and power have been left untouched and that New Labour will do anything to appease 'enterprise' and the 'free market'.

The contradiction between what people expected and what they have received has led to a political and ideological crisis among Labour supporters. Some of it takes the form of bitter humour, as in the letter to *The Guardian* which suggested that the campaign song for the next election should be 'Things Can Only Get Better'. But increasingly it takes the form of protest and argument. People are leaving Labour, not joining it. Many longstanding activists are saying they will not stand as councillors or canvass for the party in this year's elections. Some are even tearing up their cards. The enthusiasm which greeted Blair's election only two years ago seems a distant memory. No one plays the best selling election night video any more and few remember the excitement of seeing the old sleaze ridden, arrogant Tories thrown out by an electorate which had been waiting impatiently for the chance. Even *Marxism Today*, the champion of Thatcherism on the left during the 1980s, has found Blair too much to stand.[1] The reasons are not hard to see. Under Tony Blair's government it has increasingly been like the old days under the Tories. In the few months since December 1998 alone there has been a severe NHS crisis, with patients lying on trolleys or travelling across country to find beds, a war in the Gulf, with Britain playing the role of uncritical supporter of the US, and a sleaze scandal which went to the heart of government and forced two ministers to resign. This was presided over by a Labour government whose prime minister staked his reputation on being untainted with the old political scandals and incompetence of the previous 18 years of Tory rule.

On the eve of election day, 1 May 1997, Tony Blair told his Sedgefield constituents that people had to use the next 24 hours to ensure that when they woke up on 2 May they were not confronted with another five years of the 'most discredited and sleazy government...it is 24 hours to save our NHS, 24 hours to give our children the education that they need, 24 hours to give hope to our young people, security to our elderly'.[2]

Many of those who voted for him could be forgiven for thinking that little has changed. There have been no perceptible improvements in hospitals, schools or public transport. In many areas they have deteriorated. The public sector workforce suffers widespread demoralisation through low pay and worsening conditions. Teachers have been subject to an ideological assault as vicious as anything under the Tories. Blamed for 'failing schools' and 'low standards', they are now facing business intervention in schools and still have to suffer under the hated Ofsted inspection regime headed by Chris Woodhead, reappointed under Labour on a much higher salary. Privatisation is being introduced into hospitals. The privatised rail bosses can ignore a crescendo of complaints with impunity, safe in the knowledge that their profits will never be seriously threatened by the government.

Some of the poorest people in Britain have found themselves under threat: old people are expected to live on the lowest pensions of any advanced capitalist country, while single parents have been the victims of scapegoating and planned benefit cuts. Council houses are being sold off to private landlords, leaving tenants with less security of tenure and higher rents. Students are faced with fees of £1,000 a year to go through higher education; the disabled and sick are having to undertake more stringent tests to qualify for benefit; and all workers are being told they will have to pay more for their future pensions. Those who want to join a trade union to improve their conditions will find that they have won far fewer concessions than the bosses from Labour's proposed employment law.

Labour has shown itself unwilling or unable to stand up to the rich and powerful. There has been no freedom of information act, food regulation proposals have been toned down to appease the big supermarkets, green traffic laws to restrict car usage have been delayed until the next parliament, and the ban on foxhunting has been abandoned. The 'right to roam' law has been subject to a similar fate under pressure from some of the most right wing people in Britain, the country landowners.

Blair justifies his policies by reference to a Third Way between right and left in politics. Both traditional poles have failed—state socialism was a disaster and neo-liberalism in economics has also brought the excesses of the market. Now Labour can position itself to the right of traditional social democracy (as represented by Old Labour) and to the right of the social democratic leaders in Europe, such as Lionel Jospin in France and Gerhard Schröder in Germany. In a recent speech Blair spelt out what the Third Way meant in terms of a centre-left consensus: that human capital matters more to economic success than money or equipment; that markets work best but need regulation; that the foundation of the modern welfare state is work for those who can and security for those who cannot; that how a government spends money and what it funds are as important as how much it spends; that a strong civic society rests on responsibilities as well as rights; and that political power should be devolved to the lowest possible level.[3] The theory of the Third Way underpins the policies which his government is pushing through and which are bringing Blair and New Labour into repeated collisions with its own members, its voters and many trade unionists. That is why, in every major area of government policy, the contradictions are becoming sharper and more problematic for Blair.

The legacy

The stock response of the Blair government to any criticism is that it takes time to repair the damage caused by 18 years of Thatcher rule. Labour voters will have to wait patiently while there are small incremental improvements in areas such as schools and hospitals and nothing can be promised until the economy is in sufficiently good shape to allow it. But the legacy of cuts and devastation caused by 18 years of Tory rule (and the Callaghan Labour government which preceded the Tories from 1976 to 1979) have left many areas of society in a terrible state. Indeed, Britain has become a land of extremes, statistically speaking. Both poverty and inequality have grown dramatically. Tax changes between 1985 and 1995 have led directly to the poorest tenth of the population being 4 percent worse off, while the richest tenth are 6 percent better off.[4] Direct tax rates as a percentage of gross domestic product in Britain are lower than in any other EU country except Portugal.[5] Between 1979 and 1995 in Britain the gap between top and bottom earnings widened by more than one third. This mirrored the growing gap in the US and New Zealand, while Japan and most Western European countries saw the differential remain more or less the same.[6] Whereas for most of the postwar period the incomes of those at different levels rose at more or less the same rate, between 1979 and 1995 this changed. Higher incomes rose much faster, with that of the richest tenth rising by 68 percent and that of the poorest tenth actually falling by 8 percent.[7] No wonder that by the early 1990s there were two and a half times as many people in poverty as there were in 1979.[8]

This stark worsening of inequality and poverty has been matched with a deterioration of public services in virtually every area. The percentage of GDP spent on health is one of the lowest in the advanced capitalist world.[9] Public transport has less money devoted to it in terms of population than virtually anywhere else in Western Europe. Expenditure on rail infrastructure per head is lower than Portugal or Spain; public transport fares in London are the highest of any European capital; fewer people use public transport than in other European countries.[10] Creeping privatisation in areas such as care of the elderly means that places in council residential homes and NHS hospitals have been cut by more than a third since the late 1970s; at the same time the number of private residential homes trebled and those in private hospitals and nursing homes have increased by five times.[11]

It is obvious that radical remedies rather than gradual reforms are needed in order to make a significant impact on these problems. Instead, Labour imitates the previous Tory polices which have proved disastrous. There is no commitment to renationalisation; public spending is being kept to previous Tory limits for the first two years of government; projects such as the modernisation of the London tube or building new hospitals are to rely on private finance; and higher taxes are not even contemplated as a means of rectifying the situation. The Blair government has prided itself on the levels of approval received from big business and the caution it has shown in altering previous government policies. The reason lies in its determination to avoid what it sees as the mistakes of past Labour governments and to follow a precise plan of government action. In practice, however, Labour has bowed to its traditional enemies in the media, big business and the middle classes. It has appointed Tories to many public positions, including overseeing reform of the House of Lords. In the process it has assured such people—many of whom would never have voted Labour—that they have nothing to fear.

At the same time Blair has alienated many of his traditional supporters by attacking all the beliefs that 'Old Labour' held dear—from comprehensive education to an NHS free at the point of use. Blair's central assumption, that getting the economy right and allowing free rein to businessmen to 'create wealth' will solve all his other problems, is increasingly prone to criticism.

Beyond boom and bust?

The Blairites always had a model for how they would run government. Drawing heavily on the successful Clinton election campaign in the US in 1992, New Labour believed it could build a successful government, running for at least two terms, which would move Labour firmly onto the centre ground of British politics and finish the Labour left (the main Blairite enemy) forever. Some of the strategy for this was frankly ridiculous. Blair's election campaign was, following Clinton, based on the profound messages: 'time for change; the failure of Bush (Major); Clinton (Blair) is young and dynamic; we offer a partnership between government and people'.[12] But the most enduring message that the Clinton campaign gave to the Blairites was its famous catchphrase, 'It's the economy, stupid'—once you get the economy right then everything else follows. Blair and his chancellor, Gordon Brown, have always taken economic success as their touchstone. Every policy proposed by Labour was 'costed' before the election; every proposal for spending has been accompanied with the proviso that it can only be achieved when the money is there. But Blair and Brown have proved themselves to be much more than simply careful keepers of the Treasury purse; their ideological commitments dictate that they embrace such methods, extend them into as many areas of public spending as they can, and make sure that they obey the wishes of the businessmen whom they admire so much.

Some of this is very Old Labour indeed—it goes back to the days of Ramsay MacDonald and his chancellor Philip Snowden in 1931, when the Labour government's commitment to following orthodox economic policies led to wage and benefit cuts and a split inside Labour as MacDonald formed a government with the Tories. But Blair and Brown's strategy is dressed up in a rejection of Old Labour 'Keynesian' methods, which in turn is justified by the increasingly global nature of capitalism. Capital is no longer anchored down or tied to nation states, the argument runs, and so there can be no regulation of capital by governments or other forms of state intervention. All that governments can do is create skilled and educated workforces, prepared to work flexibly to suit the demands of global capital, which can only be subject to minimal controls or regulation—for example, a minimum wage, but one set at a sufficiently low rate so as not to deter capital. Tax and wage rates have to be 'competitive' in order to attract investment; hence the boast that corporation tax is one of the lowest in the world and the refusal to consider raising the very low rates of tax on higher earners. Wages and conditions for British workers are some of the lowest of the Western European countries, and the Blair government has consistently refused to raise them to match those of German or French workers.

This strategy demands an almost total acceptance of the workings of the free market. If workers accept low enough wages they will see unemployment falling. The only way to prevent factory closures is for the workforce to be sufficiently flexible that the company does not move abroad. The excessively long working hours of most British workers, which became commonplace under Thatcher and Major, have to be accepted in the name of flexibility.[13] The answer to those forced to exist on low benefits is that they should go back to work. Since he became Labour leader, Blair has consistently followed this line of argument. Indeed, as his leadership progressed he increasingly came to publicly favour the 'Anglo-American' completely deregulated model of capitalism against the 'Rhineland' model with its greater employers' costs and more regulated system of employment. The logic of following the markets meant heaping praise on the Asian Tigers, seen until the economic crisis there during 1997 as the fastest growing and most successful economies in the world, and praising the epitome of deregulated capitalism, Rupert Murdoch. Blair even travelled to Australia to address a conference of NewsCorp Murdoch executives in 1995.

During his election campaign, Blair went out of his way to appease big business—an opening election broadcast featured Terence Conran, Gerry Robinson and Anita Roddick.[14] He spoke at the Corn Exchange in the City of London on 7 April 1997 where, although he called for a Third Way between laissez faire capitalism and state control, in practice this meant tax cuts, flexible labour markets and an assumption that 'economic activity is best left to the private sector' and the 'postwar Keynesian dream is well and truly buried.' Days later he stressed, in a business manifesto, an inflation target of 2.5 percent, tough rules on borrowing and spending, public-private finance for transport, and education improvement to increase skills. A letter to *The Times* by 84 businessmen stated that business could 'look forward with confidence to a profitable future with a Labour government'.[15]

The economic rectitude continued after the election, with Gordon Brown promising that public spending would remain within the narrow limits laid down by the Tories for the next two years. Spending could not be financed through higher taxation but only through real growth and expansion of the economy, which alone would allow better health, education and transport. There was one fatal flaw in the argument: if the economy failed to expand then public spending would be slashed further, more people would become unemployed and would have to exist on inadequate benefits, there would be no room for improvement in living standards. Brown dealt with this by boasting that Britain would be able to turn its back on boom and bust—an easy boast since Labour took office when the economy was growing, unemployment was relatively low and expansion of public spending looked a possibility after the two years of strict Tory spending controls. However, it became clear throughout 1998 and in early 1999 that avoidance of bust would be no easy matter.

There was, first of all, the recession and economic crisis already hitting so much of the world economy. At first it was commonplace among Western economists and politicians to assume that the severe financial, economic and social crises which devastated several of the Asian Tigers from mid-1997 onwards would not affect the Western economies. They saw huge devaluations in countries such as Thailand and Indonesia, and the collapse of banks and financial institutions in countries as important economically as Japan, but believed that 'the contagion' could be contained. This changed in August 1998 with the collapse of the Russian economy, which led to massive losses against a devalued rouble, when even the billionaire speculator George Soros could see that all was not rosy for the future of capitalism.[16] Catastrophe beckoned again following the near demise of the hedge fund Long Term Capital Management, which nearly caused a collapse on Wall Street and did for a time herald a 'flight to cash' as investors even shied away from government bonds, believing that the markets were going haywire. The devaluation of the Brazilian currency, the real, in early 1999 upset temporarily stabilised money markets and once again raised prospects of world recession. There is still debate about whether the whole world will enter recession, or whether the US and parts of Western Europe will escape it. But already between a third and two fifths of the world are in recession; the world's second largest economy, Japan, is in deep and seemingly intractable crisis and there are signs of slowdown in the US economy.[17]

There is general agreement that the British economy, for once in a favourable situation when a Labour government took office, is heading towards recession. There is still disagreement about how bad this will be.[18] Towards the end of 1998 there was much anecdotal evidence of a serious recession: decline of manufacturing output, the beginning of signs of recession in services, and an apparently catastrophic slump in many areas of consumer spending. Although the fall in levels of unemployment recorded early in 1999 led some to believe that a recession could be avoided, this seems unlikely. Economic growth is slowing down: 'The economy has slowed to a crawl. Government statisticians say that the economy grew by only 0.2 percent in the last quarter of 1998...some economists expect it to be revised to an even lower figure later. Most forecasters expect paltry growth in the first half of this year'.[19] The article continues, 'Most economists think Mr Brown's forecast of 1 percent growth this year is too rosy'.[20] Whether the economy manages a 'soft landing' or whether the recession is much harder, the squeeze on delivering the public services which Gordon Brown insists can only be achieved by getting the economy right will be much more severe. Brown is committed to a golden rule that current spending cannot exceed tax revenues over the business cycle. With a recession, more will be spent in areas such as welfare benefits and less will be received in tax revenues. Although the Treasury hopes that this will even itself out over the cycle—that downturn in the economy will be followed relatively quickly by upturn which will reverse this process—there is no certainty that this will happen, thus leading to the Blair government holding down or cutting public spending further.

Blair also faces a dilemma over entry into the euro. He is caught between pressure from the majority of the capitalist class who clearly want Britain to enter sooner rather than later, and the Murdoch press which is opposed and which so far Blair has avoided antagonising. The pressure on him to hold a referendum quickly will grow, since he is now being criticised by big business for not joining straight after the election. Either way, he risks unpopularity since public opinion is still against the single currency and Blair may find himself under much greater attack from both sides.

New Labour, new means tests

While Labour refuses to intervene to regulate the economy or to curb the excesses of big business, it has no such qualms about intervening to direct the lives of individuals. Blair and Brown's determination to abide by a degree of financial rectitude is matched by a level of social authoritarianism with regard to welfare which apes the policies of their Tory predecessors but manages a degree of sanctimoniousness which goes beyond what even many Tories would have dared. Whether in praise of adoption for children born outside marriage or opposing parents who take their children on holiday in term time, Labour ministers are never short of a quote about parental responsibility. There are constant attempts to police the family, council estates and schools. This attitude marks a move away from society taking collective responsibility for social problems and towards individuals themselves carrying a much greater burden. It is not a new development: the long term trend since the Callaghan government of the late 1970s has been to shift the burden of care away from the state and towards individuals. There has been a huge shift away from state and towards private care for the elderly; council housing has been progressively privatised, at first piecemeal, but now in huge blocks of housing stock, and in the process the subsidy on housing has moved from bricks and mortar to effectively paying private landlords; the costs of education and healthcare have been stealthily pushed onto the individual through payment for 'extra curricular' activities in schools, tuition fees and loans for students, and charges for eye tests, dentistry and prescriptions. But now working people suffering from these cuts in public services are also blamed for their problems.

The accompanying talk of 'rights and responsibilities' claims that rewards in society come from taking a responsible part in society. Blair draws heavily on the ideas of community and social justice but his use of the terms do not imply an egalitarian philosophy. Rather they suggest one where the solutions to problems rest very much with the individual rather than with society as a whole. In this, they represent a return to Victorian liberalism: if, despite the state's efforts, people remain unemployed, then this is their own fault and reflects their own inadequacies. Since individuals are therefore responsible for their own unemployment, punitive measures are justified. The attempt at an ideological justification for such policies involves a rejection of the principles of the universal welfare state established after the Second World War. The principle was that everyone in a position to do so paid tax and national insurance contributions and in return received benefits when they were sick, old or in need of education. In practice this has worked as a 'savings bank'—the money paid in tends to be received in benefits by the same people (so the young and healthy pay contributions and receive them back when they are old or sick), the majority of welfare benefits therefore being self-financed. Nonetheless, there is an element of redistribution from the richest to the poorest involved in this principle as the richer tend to pay more tax while the poorer tend to receive more benefits. A recent study concludes that if public services were paid for by user charges rather than through taxation, losses to the poorest households would average £5,000 a year while gains to the richest households would average £11,000 a year. The introduction of means tested benefits would only increase benefits traps and disincentives to work.[21]

Far from helping redistribution the Blairite project on welfare requires abandoning the whole idea. Instead, he wants a system where the vast majority in work pay more, often for private provision, while state benefits remain an inadequate safety net. The tax cuts for the rich instituted under the Tories have been upheld by Labour, on the grounds that people will not pay more taxes (even though there is overwhelming poll evidence to the contrary). Instead a lower tax regime is supposed to be accompanied by higher individual spending on private pensions, on higher education, and if individuals 'choose' to do so on private education and healthcare. The element of compulsion suggested in the plan for second pensions for all British workers is effectively the further partial privatisation of taxation and benefits. Blair rejects the Thatcherite notion that 'there is no such thing as society', but his view of society rests heavily on the individual within it and has a profoundly conservative tinge: 'The only way to rebuild social order and stability is through strong values, socially shared, inculcated through individuals, family, government and the institutions of civil society'.[22]

The role of individual effort in the context of the family is also stressed in his view that social justice is about effort to improve one's situation rather than changing society so that everyone can be levelled up, summed up in the phrase that Labour should strive not for equality of outcome but for equality of opportunity. This idea puts the burden on individuals not to fail rather than on society not to fail them. It also reinforces the notion that society is made up of a majority of discerning consumers whose lives are one happy round of choosing how to spend their money and who want to pick and choose education or healthcare in the same way as buying a pair of shoes. These public services therefore have to be geared to a series of costly and time wasting tables and standards, rather than seriously trying to raise the standards of public services in all areas and for everyone regardless of 'consumer demand'. And for those unfortunates who do not fit into this model of consumer society, then New Labour has shown itself to be as arrogant, unsympathetic and authoritarian as any previous government.

Neil Kinnock once said of the Tory government: 'I warn you not to get sick. I warn you not to be old.' One could equally warn under this Labour government not to be young and unemployed, or living on a sink estate, or to be old and poor, or to get into trouble with the police. If you are a single mother or sick or disabled and on benefits, then the government pressurises you to get a job. If you live on a poor estate, then the government pressurises you to allow a private landlord to take over. If you are an asylum seeker you will be denied benefits and any means of earning a living, and threatened with harassment and deportation. If you break the law then you can expect zero tolerance. Yet there is no sign that these policies work. Many of them are taken from Blair's hero, Bill Clinton. Yet the US's low levels of unemployment are based on a low wage, deregulated economy which has already created widespread discontent among workers even in a boom. It also contains the highest prison population in the world—a costly way, both financially and socially, of avoiding welfare. And the abolition of many social welfare benefits there, plus the restriction of many more, will have devastating consequences for millions when unemployment rises.

The centrepiece of government welfare policy is Welfare to Work. In 1994 Gordon Brown spelt out the thinking behind it:

We must look hard at our own welfare system to ensure that it provides pathways out of unemployment and poverty rather than trapping people in persistent dependency. For the risks and insecurities that the welfare state was set up to combat have changed dramatically over 50 years and the welfare state has to keep up with the times. The welfare state must be about supporting people as they respond to these challenges—extending their choices and opportunities: acting as a trampoline rather than as a safety net.[23]

The idea of giving people who are at present 'socially excluded' the skills and the motivation to earn a wage and therefore to stop their dependency on the state is central to Welfare to Work. Yet it begs a number of questions. Many people cannot work for reasons of age, health or disability: these people are now condemned to a miserable existence on benefits which barely cover the essentials of life. Many others who are at present on benefits will almost certainly work in the future. This is true statistically of both the young unemployed and of single parents on benefit. Yet Labour is insisting that such people are pressurised or even forced to take work at very low wages which, far from developing their skills, is often the most routine work which cannot attract a stable workforce at normal pay rates. Education is likely to be further disbarred to such people since it now carries very high costs up front in the form of fees and loans, which many people on benefits will see no way of repaying and so will be deterred from such a course. In addition, Welfare to Work has not been an unqualified success in the US or Australia, where it has already been tried. The Australian JET programme cost taxpayers more after five years than it had saved because it involved a subsidy to employers. Existing workers are often displaced by these subsidised workers who have to accept lower wages, so the number of new jobs created has not been particularly high. There are also worries that such schemes do not represent the first rung on a ladder to well paid work, but a revolving door between low skill, low reward jobs and the dole queue. Most importantly, there is no guarantee; the scheme is predicated on an expanding economy—what if there are no jobs?[24]

There is no doubt that the government wants to increase the level of compulsion in Welfare to Work. In 1997 Gordon Brown introduced the scheme in his budget by stressing the responsibilities of young unemployed people: 'With these new opportunities for young people come new responsibilities. There will be no fifth option—to stay at home on full benefit. So when they sign on for benefit they will be signing up for work.' In effect there is little difference between this and the 'Workfare' schemes which Labour has traditionally rejected—as recently as in 1994 in the Commission on Social Justice—because of the element of compulsion. But 'if Workfare means certain categories of the unemployed having to work for their benefits, then Welfare to Work is a form of Workfare'.[25]

Yet this level of authoritarianism has already created a backlash, especially in terms of the proposed compulsion towards single parents or the disabled to find work. Although the government was forced to retreat on its plans to slash benefits in such areas in the wake of major disagreement and protest around the 'welfare roadshows', and although the unpopularity of these measures led directly to the departure of the ministers responsible, Harriet Harman and Frank Field, in July 1998, there are repeated attempts to try to introduce an element of compulsion. This, plus the holding down of benefits to extremely low levels which have a demoralising and harmful effect on claimants, has led to a general sense that New Labour is not prepared to do anything to help some of the poorest and most needy. Indeed, it is more likely to blame them for their problems. This feeling has led to a level of militancy among groups such as pensioners and the disabled which has only grown under Blair's government and which is unlikely to be appeased by any minor changes in policy. Welfare to Work has bred discontent and a degree of cynicism about Labour's shabby treatment of the unemployed, but has yet to generate significant organised protests. The advent of a recession and higher levels of unemployment might change that; it would certainly expose both the harshness and the inadequacy of Labour's welfare policy which relies on market provision.[26]

Democracy and constitutional change

The manifesto on which Labour was elected in 1997 contained a profound commitment to constitutional change. Scotland and Wales would be allowed a degree of devolution; regions in England would receive more power; there would be elected mayors in London and other cities. Labour was pledged to abolition of voting rights for hereditary peers in the House of Lords, a referendum on electoral reform and a freedom of information law. Government would be more in the control of the people, less corrupt and sleazy, and more locally accessible. Blair sees this area of constitutional politics as very important in delivering what he regards as true democracy and in modernising the British state. While he has introduced legislation to achieve many of these changes, and constitutional change is heralded as a Blairite success story, in reality there have been a number of setbacks and reverses for those wanting such reform. Freedom of information legislation has been put on hold, much to the disgruntlement of many Labour supporters, as has some local government reform. House of Lords reform has become bogged down in compromise. A referendum on changing the voting system to a form of proportional representation has been deferred. Most importantly, the supposed benefits to Labour of Scottish and Welsh devolution and of a London mayor have turned into their opposite, as Blair increasingly acts as someone who believes in democracy as long as everyone agrees with him.

This is most obvious in Scotland and Wales. The theory behind devolution was that it would allow more local accountability. It would also pre-empt calls from the nationalists for complete independence by allowing a degree of local decision making. Despite the failure of the devolution referenda in the late 1970s, this time Labour would organise devolution votes based on a simple voting majority and would be strongly placed to dominate the Scottish Parliament and the Welsh Assembly. At first there was little doubt that Labour would benefit electorally from these changes. The Tories were completely wiped out in May 1997, retaining no seats in either Scotland or Wales. In both, the nationalists were in second place electorally at the general election but neither the Scottish National Party nor Plaid Cymru made an electoral breakthrough: the SNP had around 22 percent share of the vote, only half a percent up on the previous election. In Wales Plaid received just under 10 percent of the vote (an increase of 1 percent) and this was heavily concentrated in the Welsh speaking and rural areas.[27]

The referenda took place just months after the election, showing a clear majority for a Scottish Parliament and an extremely narrow one— 0.6 percent—for the Welsh Assembly. However, far from the referenda satisfying demands for greater control in Scotland and Wales, the political result was an increase in support for independence. This was fuelled in Scotland even before the referendum when the Blairites hedged over the question of tax raising powers for the parliament. In the 18 months or so since, however, the Labour Party in Scotland has been under repeated attack and has seen its support fall to the benefit of the SNP. Arguments over the blatant selection of Blairites as candidates for the parliament, while many respected Labour figures were passed over, has led to divisions in the party and a number of defections to the SNP locally. Blairite

MP Rosemary McKenna, chair of the selection board, claimed that 'we could not stuff our lists full of second rate hacks and expect Labour voters to express blind loyalty to the party.' In fact the second raters include two MPs, the former secretary to the Scottish party and the former leader of Edinburgh City Council.[28]

There are already signs of a backlash against this behaviour. Labour has lost a number of council by-elections to the SNP. The veteran Westminster MP Dennis Canavan has been denied a Labour nomination for a Scottish Parliament seat and is now standing as an independent. Labour's continuation of Tory policies has alienated many of its supporters. For example, it has used openly Tory arguments to accuse the SNP of preparing a 'tax bombshell' for Scottish voters. The journalist John Lloyd has complained that devolution has been 'an anti-English project'. But, as Joyce McMillan, writing in *The Scotsman,* said, the feeling for greater independence has little to do with anti-English sentiment and a lot to do with Blair's policies—the 'over-enthusiastic endorsement of Margaret Thatcher's "no alternative" approach to market economics, which once again has left Scots of the left with no utopia to dream of except a Scottish one'.[29]

Although there appeared to be less concern over devolution in Wales, with the very narrow yes vote and the fewer powers devolved to the Welsh Assembly, the rows involving Labour over the assembly have become as sharp as those in Scotland in the run up to elections in May 1999. There was pressure from the Blairites to ensure that Ron Davies, the Secretary of State for Wales, won the nomination as Labour leader of the assembly against the strong challenge of Rhodri Morgan. Morgan, although far from being a left winger, was regarded as unreliable by Blair and with the help of the union block vote was eventually defeated. The nightmare scenario arose after Davies was forced to resign following the 'Clapham Common incident'. Blair's replacement as Welsh secretary was Alun Michael and he insisted that Michael should also lead the assembly. This was seen as the imposition of a London Blairite candidate on Wales and came on top of a series of events which had alienated many Labour voters from Blair. By-elections in council seats earlier in 1998 demonstrated a shift away from Labour in one of its strongest heartlands towards Plaid Cymru, which appeared a more left wing alternative. In summer 1998 Plaid took its first seat on Swansea council for over 20 years and Plaid won a 'safe' Labour seat near Bridgend.[30] Support appears to be growing for Plaid not just in its traditional areas but in the industrial valleys of south Wales where Labour is dominant.

Rhodri Morgan's challenge to Alun Michael has led to civil war inside Labour. There is near universal discontent with Michael and with Blair. Had the election been based on one member one vote of the Welsh

Labour Party membership, then Morgan would have won hands down. But Blair had to abandon his supposedly favoured method of election and insisted on an electoral college with only one third of the votes going to individual members; trade unions made up another third, and MPs plus some assembly candidates the final third. Even so, the vote was very close and Michael won thanks to the union block vote which delivered for Blair against the wishes of many union members. Blair breathed a sigh of relief when Michael won, but his relief is won at the cost of delivering more votes to Plaid in May and of uproar in the Welsh party. The forced imposition of Michael resulted in an own goal for Blair.

New Labour faces a similar dilemma in London. The idea of an elected mayor and a partly elected quango to run London was a compromise. Abolition of the old Greater London Council under Ken Livingstone was very unpopular, but Blair had no desire to restore a similar body. He would like the mayor to be business friendly and firmly New Labour. Unfortunately for him most Londoners both in and outside the Labour Party think differently. Ken Livingstone is by far the most popular figure for mayor and would be the obvious choice—except that Blair opposes him. Labour's intention is therefore to exclude him from any shortlist. Yet it is obvious that Livingstone is popular precisely because he represents something to the left of Blair in a city where many local issues such as transport and environment are highly politicised, where the swing to Labour in the 1997 election was higher than the average nationally and where even many of the suburban outer London seats returned Labour MPs. There have been a series of desperate attempts to find Blair-friendly alternatives to Livingstone, so far with little success. The latest signs are that Blair will try to persuade health minister Frank Dobson to stand, on the grounds that he could beat Livingstone in a shortlist election of London party members. But this is a risky strategy—as in south Wales, it depends on party members voting as Blair wants, and there is no guarantee of this. The alternative is to exclude Livingstone from the shortlist altogether—the favoured Blair method, but one which contradicts his professions of democracy.

Labour's policy on the House of Lords has undergone progressive erosion under Blair. When he became leader, party policy was the abolition of the existing institution and its replacement with a second elected chamber. This began to change in 1996, when Blair's John Smith Memorial Lecture substituted instead the abolition of the hereditary principle: 'Surely we should first make the House of Lords a genuine body of the distinguished and meritorious—with a better, more open and independent means of establishing membership—and then debate how we incorporate democratic accountability'.[31] Consequently Labour's manifesto promised to abolish the voting rights of hereditary peers in the House of Lords as 'the first stage in a process of reform to make the House of Lords more democratic and representative'. However, since the revolt of the Tory peers even this has been abandoned. Blair has compromised, allowing 91 hereditaries to remain. Labour ministers now claim that a fully elected second house is impossible because it would clash with the Commons and the whole question has been left to a royal commission. The likelihood of any change in this parliament is becoming more remote and Labour's policy, far from being radical or threatening the status quo, 'is open to the accusation that what is proposed is a giant quango in the sense that all members will be appointed'.[32]

A similar fate has befallen the campaigns for a change in the voting system to a form of proportional representation (PR). This is an issue which deeply divides the Labour Party right up to cabinet level. Several of the most powerful ministers such as Gordon Brown and Jack Straw are opposed to any change in the electoral system. Blair is claiming that he has not made up his mind on the issue; but his appointment of the Liberal peer Lord Jenkins to head the 'independent' commission on what form the new voting system should take gives some idea of his real sympathies. The Jenkins commission which reported in October 1998 recommended the 'alternative vote plus' system of PR, a system which would benefit the Liberal Democrats probably more than any other party. Indeed, the various forms of PR being implemented already in Scotland and Wales and proposed for the Westminster parliament are all aimed at strengthening the centre parties (and the Tory party which has no seats in Scotland and Wales) rather than allowing real minority voices. Electoral reform is therefore central to the policies of the Liberal Democrats but many Labour MPs have greater doubts. The Welsh Office minister Peter Hain has come out publicly against the Jenkins proposals, saying that only the alternative vote should be implemented without the 'plus' element of MPs elected by a top up system across the regions, which should be delayed for ten years. 'I...doubt whether MPs would vote themselves out of their seats just like that,' said Hain.[33] Although there are many who support various forms of PR on the basis that there would be MPs from all main parties sitting in every area, and who therefore see it as enhancing democracy, the proposals on offer seem likely strengthen the centre based coalition politics of which Blair is so fond.[34] He knows that he is in a minority on this question inside his party and that it can become one of Labour's major divisions—in a way which, so far, economic policy has not been—and therefore the referendum on voting reform has again been pushed into a second term.

There must be ruling class worries about the piecemeal way in which Blair is approaching reform. The deal with the Tories over the hereditary peers meant that the reformed second chamber suddenly became a much more immediate prospect, but without any real thought about the political or constitutional implications. This is an example of how Blair is casually restructuring the state in ways which can create all sorts of problems of coherence and co-ordination.

Tony's friends

When considering the factors which have led to the growth in cynicism about Blair's government, it is impossible to ignore the individuals chosen by him to help implement his policies. Blair's appointees and their behaviour speak volumes about the values and priorities of the government and of Blair himself. Despite the fine talk of May 1997, the Labour government has been noted for a level of high living, sleaze and corruption affecting Labour ministers in the way which has been traditionally true of the Tories. In addition, an astonishing number of those hostile to traditional Labour values have been rewarded with often highly lucrative posts in and around government.

By far the most serious case of sleaze involved that of the two ministers forced to resign at Christmas 1998. Peter Mandelson had received a secret loan of £373,000 from another minister, the Paymaster General Geoffrey Robinson. The loan had been kept secret, allegedly even from Blair, until it was leaked to *The Guardian* newspaper. Mandelson rapidly resigned when the press turned against him. The implications of the case were clear to Labour supporters. Mandelson is the architect of the whole New Labour project, was the closest to Blair in the cabinet (to which he was only promoted last summer), and was the most keen to cultivate new friends among the rich, powerful and right wing—these ranged from Rupert Murdoch's daughter Elisabeth to Camilla Parker Bowles and Carla Powell, the right wing Tory socialite. It was to entertain such people that he used the loan to buy himself a half million pound house in London's Notting Hill.

As a consequence of these qualities, Mandelson is the most hated man inside the Labour Party. He failed to win a place on Labour's National Executive Committee (NEC) in 1997, despite Blair's backing, and was instead beaten by the left winger Ken Livingstone. When it was suggested soon after his resignation that he would return to cabinet within the current parliament there was uproar in the Parliamentary Labour Party. There has still been no adequate explanation of how Mandelson has financed his expensive lifestyle on an MP's salary.

His departure is damaging for Blair who relied on him as a loyal and determined ally. His departure also raises further questions of sleaze. The most serious previous allegation was about the Formula One racing boss

Bernie Ecclestone, who donated £1 million to Labour before the election and was coincidentally exempted from the ban on tobacco advertising. Other notorious cases of New Labour's dubious connections include that of Derek Draper, the lobbyist and friend of Mandelson who boasted of his unique access to government: 'There are 17 people who count. To say that I am intimate with every one of them is the understatement of the century'.[35] Draper has since been publicly shunned by his former intimates, although he is confident enough to appear in the media. Others have been more fortunate. Tim Allan, former Blair press adviser in Downing Street, is now a boss of Murdoch's BSkyB. Benjamin Wegg-Prosser, adviser to Peter Mandelson, rapidly found new employment as assistant to the editor of Murdoch's *Sun*.

It is hardly news that Blair is friendly to big business. Long before the election he said:

> *I think one of the great changes that has happened in the whole Labour culture is to recognise that we need entrepreneurs and people who are going to go out and be wealth creators and who are going to become wealthy by their own efforts. I support that, I want that, a successful economy needs that.*[36]

But the scale of businessmen's involvement in government and its entourage and Blair's sheer enthusiasm for businessmen surprised many people. Far from these people showing entrepreneurship or obtaining effective results, several of the most prominent have been dismal failures. Many of them have also become tarnished. Geoffrey Robinson, a multi-millionaire businessman who was supposed to bring his acumen to government, has been forced out of office by the Mandelson loan scandal, but was already subject to other sleaze allegations. Martin Taylor, brought in as a government adviser on low pay and benefits, was last year forced out as head of Barclays Bank. Bob Ayling, boss of British Airways and a Blairite, is under increasing criticism over BA's loss of market share and for his abortive attack on workers who went on strike in the summer of 1997. Richard Branson, filmed with Blair just before the election on a Virgin train, has presided over an ever worsening train service and a similar decline in his reputation.

It is also noticeable how many Tories have gained jobs through Blair's appointments, from David Mellor to Lord Wakeham. But the most revealing of Blair's new found friends, however, lie within the ranks of his advisers and policymakers—where former members of the Social Democratic Party and the Liberal Party have found a new and comfortable home advising New Labour. These include Roger Liddle, founder member of the SDP and friend of Peter Mandelson (co-authoring *The Blair Revolution*). Liddle is an adviser to Blair on Europe and defence. Former SDP founder member Derek Scott advises Blair on economics at 10 Downing Street; former Liberal Democrat councillor and parliamentary candidate Andrew Adonis is also at Number Ten advising Blair on education. Liddle's wife, Caroline Thomson, is the daughter of Liberal peer Lord Thomson of Monifieth, a former Labour cabinet minister. She is also the former PA to Lord Jenkins of Hillhead, founder of the SDP and now a Liberal Democrat peer.

There are further connections between several of these individuals and the disgraced lobbyist Derek Draper through the lobbying consultant GPC Market Access (formerly Prima Europe). Prima Europe was founded by SDP founder Lord Taverne, chaired by former SDP founder Sir Ian Wrigglesworth and directed by Roger Liddle. Draper himself became a director of the company, pocketing £250,000 when it was bought out by GPC. Mandelson was a former consultant to Prima Europe.[37]

The SDP was constituted in 1981 with the express purpose of wrecking the Labour Party. Labour's especially disastrous vote in the 1983 election occurred because the SDP split the vote of traditional Labour supporters. The effect was Thatcher's continued rule throughout the 1980s on a minority of the vote. Despite the SDP talking about 'breaking the mould' and 'new' politics, as Labour recovered politically it collapsed, merging into the Liberal Democrats. It is a final irony that many of its luminaries seem to be some of those closest to Tony Blair politically, and that they have more influence on government than they could ever have done under their own banner. The same is true of the Liberal Democrats. The party's share of the vote fell in 1997 for the third election in a row: 'at 17.2 percent it was the party's second worst performance since it started fighting elections on a nationwide basis in February 1974'.[38]

This has not stopped Tony Blair urging closer links with the Liberal Democrats. Indeed, it has emerged that Blair was ready to offer Paddy Ashdown and other Liberal Democrats seats in the cabinet; he was only prevented from doing so by the scale of Labour's landslide which made it politically impossible for him to pursue any type of coalition. Following the announcement of his resignation in January this year, Ashdown revealed that Blair was ready to do a deal: 'a closer election [result] would have made it more possible'.[39] Peter Mandelson's close friend, the millionaire author Robert Harris, who spent election night with Blair, confirmed this when he said, 'It does appear to have been Mr Blair's intention, on the eve of Labour's election victory, to offer Mr Ashdown a cabinet seat; and it does appear to have been Mr Ashdown's intention, on the morning after, following a hasty consultation with his senior colleagues, to accept it'.[40]

If the political realities of 2 May 1997 prevented Blair and Ashdown
from taking this step, Blair has remained a fervent advocate of closer
links and possible unity between the two parties. Speaking to the Labour
Party conference only months after his landslide victory, he made clear
that not only did he want to continue his courtship of the Liberal
Democrats, but that he rejected the very basis on which the Labour Party
was formed at the beginning of the 20th century. When Blair listed his
heroes in his conference speech, he stressed:

> [they] *aren't just Ernie Bevin, Nye Bevan and Attlee. They are also Keynes,
> Beveridge, Lloyd George. Division among radicals almost 100 years ago
> resulted in a 20th century dominated by Conservatives. I want the 21st
> century to be the century of the radicals.*[41]

There is little wonder that this approach is so isolated inside the
Labour Party. Labour's roots as a party which would represent the trade
unions—or rather the trade union bureaucracy—in parliament developed
from a rejection of the Liberal Party (traditionally looked to by many
workers in the second half of the 19th century) as simply being a bosses'
party. The whole history of the struggle for working people's representation in parliament and the eventual election of the first Labour
government in 1924 was one of rejection of coalition with the Liberals.
Even when Ramsay MacDonald and Keir Hardie did make an election
deal with the Liberals, they were forced to do so secretly.[42] For Blair to
want to return to open alliances with the Liberals as part of his 'project'
is effectively to wipe out any independent history of Labour throughout
the 20th century—something which even many right wing Labour politicians cannot stomach.

Blair's isolation following the demise of Mandelson and Ashdown has
been reinforced by the obviously strong reaction to further links with the
Liberal Democrats inside the Parliamentary Labour Party and the cabinet
itself. While Ashdown claimed that the Liberal Democrats would be in
government after the next election, this was rebutted by the deputy prime
minister John Prescott when he said, 'I don't think I need anybody else…
The Labour Party carrying out its promises with a majority of 170 can well
do that'.[43] Minutes of an internal Labour Party meeting between Blair and
six representatives of the Parliamentary Labour Party in early January
revealed that he was subject to a stormy attack because of failure to consult
over closer Lib-Lab co-operation. Blair was forced to admit that 'if there
were ever any plans to extend the nature of the relationship into new territory, he would discuss these matters first with colleagues'.[44] There is
clearly a split over these issues at the top of the Labour Party between
Blair and his acolytes who want to destroy Labour and replace it with a

party incorporating the mainstream Liberal Democrats and right wing Labourites, and the majority of the cabinet, who may accept modernising policies but who are still Labourist politically. This line up is potentially highly destabilising.

It is hard to see where Blair is going over his planned closer links with the Liberal Democrats. He has lost his main ally in the cabinet, Mandelson; the Liberal Democrats' new leader after Ashdown is likely to be less amenable; there is widespread opposition among the grassroots of both parties to closer ties. Elections this year are likely to sharpen divisions between the parties. Finally there is no objective necessity with such a huge Labour majority. Therefore Blair's hands are likely to be tied until the next election. This puts a hole in his 'project' of moving to the centre ground in politics. It is unnecessary to fully agree with the ultra-Blairite Robert Harris who says 'it may well be the greatest mistake of Tony Blair's premiership—maybe even his entire career—will turn out to be his failure to keep his nerve and make Paddy Ashdown a member of his cabinet two years ago',[45] to accept that Blair's isolation in this respect is a bitter blow to him and serves to increasingly demonstrate how little support he has for these policies within his own party.

A further recent speech by Ashdown shed more light on Blair's intentions when Ashdown claimed that the prime minister's secret ambition was to see Labour split in two with left wing MPs breaking away to form their own party. Ashdown said that under the existing voting system 'a breakaway of the left is not impossible. They could be pushed into it, for Mr Blair would not miss them. But it could only come from desperation as it would be electorally doomed.' On the other hand, under PR the left would have a better electoral chance and so would split. 'New Labour would be liberated and the left would have a voice again. No more internal appeasement, no more loveless marriage'.[46] This is no doubt the authentic voice of Blair's 'project' but one which will have little resonance among Labour MPs or the wider membership, and shows how far Blair's interests diverge from mainstream Labour.

Where's the opposition?

Blair's political isolation from his party is in many ways quite marked. Very few leading Labour Party members subscribe to the 'project', and on the ground among Labour activists it has even less support. The New Labour ideologues are very small in number: they comprise the large number of Blair advisers, a minority of MPs, especially concentrated among the new intake, councillors in areas such as the London boroughs of Lambeth and Islington who are implementing major attacks on local people (and whose unpopularity denotes the massive class polarisation in these and similar boroughs), and the substantial penumbra of Westminster, Whitehall and Millbank lobbyists, advisers and researchers. The bulk of Labour MPs and activists have welcomed Blair as the first successful leader for decades, but would probably be happier with more 'Old Labour' policies and less rabid commitment to the market. Yet it is remarkable how little opposition there is to Labour from within its ranks or within the trade union leadership.

Firstly, there is the weakness of Old Labour itself. Its ethos is identified most strongly with the 1945-1951 Labour governments. At least for the first three years of that government Labour did deliver substantial reforms. This was the era of the NHS, established in 1948 despite opposition; the welfare state, which brought in a range of benefits for the old, sick and unemployed; and the nationalisation of key industries such as coal and rail, already under government control in wartime. The radical impetus of the war led to the Labour victory in 1945 and a sense that much had to change—there could be no return to the days of unemployment in the 1930s. Even during this government, however, change was very slow and often the government backed down before vested interests. So, for example, the government backed down when blocked by the House of Lords over the abolition of capital punishment, despite a narrow Commons majority.[47] And the plans for building a new society were thwarted, abandoned and curtailed as the government went on. So a survey of building on new London housing estates carried out in 1952 showed that only one nursery school out of a planned 46 had been built, only six infant welfare clinics out of a planned 26 and no health centres out of a planned 33 had been built.[48]

Nonetheless, most Labour voters believed that great changes were being achieved. Labour's 1945 manifesto said, 'The Labour Party is a socialist party, and proud of it', although it warned that 'socialism cannot come overnight, as the product of a weekend revolution'.[49] Labour supporters believed that their path to reform was on course and they were part of a mass party. Although the Labour government effectively ran out of steam by the late 1940s, and 13 years of Tory rule began in 1951 (despite Labour winning more votes in that election), the 1945 government ushered in an era of consensus politics, made possible by the expansion of the economy during the long boom of the 1950s and early 1960s. Harold Wilson's governments from 1964 to 1970 were much weaker in terms of reform than the 1945 government. However, they did preside over various changes in the law on employment such as equal pay for women. They also allowed parliamentary time for private member's bills such as the legalisation of abortion and homosexuality which brought substantial advances. There was race relations legislation, although this was extremely weak.

However, the limited reforms available to Labour in a boom were running out, as the Wilson government faced economic slowdown and industrial unrest. The nadir of Old Labour came in 1976 under James Callaghan when Labour abandoned any pretence at maintaining the post-war consensus in the face of economic crisis. The IMF demanded huge cuts in response to a bailout for the falling pound. As Gregory Elliott says, 'The day the pound nearly died portended the day British post-war social democracy, already terminally ill, did die—by its own hand'.[50] Anthony Crosland, leading right wing intellectual of post-war Labourism, was moved to say, 'Even if the government survives, does it make such a difference if Labour measures can't be implemented?'[51]

Since then the demise of Old Labour has accompanied the demise of all it stood for; it has made repeated and regular concessions and capitulations to Thatcherism and now to Blairism on the ground that the only important question was getting a Labour government elected. It now accepts privatisation, attacks on welfare and high levels of unemployment—exactly the reverse of what it once believed. Yet this desperation to make concessions to the right has only led to further concessions and to widespread demoralisation among Old Labour supporters. It is this which contributes to the crisis of Labourism at the grassroots. While Old Labour MPs take seats in the House of Lords, those in the Old Labour heartlands who have spent time, sometimes decades, canvassing and working for the Labour Party now find themselves marginalised and ignored by the government for which they spent 18 years waiting. This is why the crisis of Labourism is at its most acute in those Old Labour areas such as south Wales, central Scotland, the north of England and inner London, and why many Labour supporters now find themselves pushed to the left.

Yet the left has not been immune from the crisis. The Labour left has never been weaker than it is now. The series of witch hunts, defeats and retreats which marked the 1980s and early 1990s under the leadership first of Neil Kinnock and then John Smith were continued under Blair. The abolition of Clause Four of the party's constitution, which contained the commitment to nationalisation, provoked little opposition. The emasculation of the left's traditional strongholds, such as the annual conference and the National Executive Committee, has occurred with little organised resistance. Local government, the stronghold of the Bennite Labour left, has been progressively weakened by legal and financial restrictions under the Tories, which are being continued under Labour. This is a policy which in effect amounts to ratecapping and includes further government and private sector intervention in areas such as education. Labour's left has been dramatically weakened organisationally. However, it has also been weakened politically and ideologically. The basis of Labour's traditional ideology was that a mixed economy with high public spending and government intervention was the most effective way of winning change and creating a fairer society with full employment and a decent welfare system. The failure of old style social democracy led to an increasing embrace of the market under successive leaders which reached its peak with Blair. However critical most Labour Party members might be of this strategy, they see no alternative. They accept the logic of electoralism which means they will agree to compromise and retreat in order to win. They argue that this then allows them to make real changes when in power. But of course being in power only leads to further retreat—in the name of electoralism. So today even many left wingers accept the need for private investment in areas such as public transport or health. When the arch-Blairite minister (and former Labour left councillor) Stephen Byers said in February that the most important thing was not wealth redistribution but wealth creation, many Labour MPs grumbled, but there was no open attack on him. The demise of the East European regimes and the collapse of the Communist Party has also had an effect, since the Labour left historically has relied heavily on the CP for its ideas. The collapse of state 'socialism' left many former Communists and Labour lefts turning towards an acceptance of the market and, therefore, many of Blair's concepts. As Paul Anderson and Nyta Mann have pointed out:

> *The parliamentary left's organisational weakness is not, however, its only problem or its biggest one. For some years, it has lacked anything like the confidence, drive or sense of direction of the Labour modernisers. The disagreements over tactics that were the original cause of the Tribune-Campaign split have been overlaid by deeper differences as the parliamentary left has grappled with—or failed to grapple with—the myriad economic, political and social changes since the early 1980s... There is no agreed left position in the PLP today on the economy, Europe, constitutional reform (particularly the electoral system), the future of the welfare state, and much else besides. Insofar as the parliamentary left has found unity of purpose in recent years, it has been in fighting unsuccessful rearguard actions against changes initiated by the party leadership—on public ownership, on defence, on the closed shop, on OMOV, on Clause Four.*[52]

The outcome of this is that the criticism from Labour's left is often inaudible, and usually makes big concessions to Blairism. Stalwarts of Old Labour such as Roy Hattersley, former deputy leader and always firmly on the right of the party, are now some of the boldest critics of Blair (at least in the columns of *The Guardian*), while many erstwhile Bennites have made their peace with Blair. Dawn Primarolo, one of Tony Benn's main supporters in Bristol and a poll tax non-payer as late as

1990, is now Paymaster General attached to the Treasury, and a full supporter of the Blair project. She said recently, 'I feel I've matured. I've been an MP for 11 years... I've learned a lot. And also the political agenda's moved on'.[53] Other ministers have a similar approach. Robin Cook, once regarded as a leader of the left, now carries out Britain's foreign policy, such as the bombing of Iraq, with apparent enthusiasm. He denies that he ever used the term 'ethical foreign policy' but refers rather to 'an ethical dimension' to foreign policy.[54] Traditional left wingers who are excluded from government office, such as Dennis Skinner or Tony Benn, are treated as mavericks or dinosaurs, allowed a certain degree of freedom to speak out because no one dares challenge them, but also dismissed as irrelevant. In any case they remain individuals with little power to influence events. The left in parliament is probably weaker than ever. Although some of this is due to the increasingly Blairite intake of MPs, it is also due to the left's political weakness. After 1997 only six new MPs out of a total of 183 new Labour MPs joined the left wing Campaign Group.[55] The former leading lights of the Tribune Group such as Peter Hain are now in government. One of the most favoured platforms for left MPs, the NEC, has now been denied them, since MPs on the committee are no longer elected by the membership but appointed by Blair. The main opposition has come from the Grassroots Alliance, several of whose members, including Liz Davies and *Tribune* editor Mark Seddon, beat the Blairite slate to win places on the NEC under the new rules in 1998. However, since then their opposition has been muted and constitutional in its approach.

In London Ken Livingstone is campaigning to run for mayor despite the bitter opposition of Blair. He is obviously banking on things going so badly for Labour in areas such as Scotland and Wales that the leadership may be faced with no alternative than to let him stand. Yet this has led him into a campaign which is confused and contradictory and where he has hesitated in putting forward really radical policies. Livingstone has repeatedly made concessions to Blair including the following in October 1997:

I haven't written off Blair and I don't think the left should. There are a lot of truly ghastly people gathered around Blair, like lice on the back of a hedgehog and they have their own agenda... They seem to regret being born in Britain because they would rather be working in the White House in Washington. Now we have nothing in common with these people. But Blair is different. When Blair became active in the Labour Party he was broadly in line with the consensus at the time.

Livingstone's analysis went further; the extremes of the left at the time were to blame for Blair's right wing development. In particular Tony Benn's speech to the 1980 Labour Party conference 'marked Benn out as too far to the left for many who had been sympathetic to him. So it cut him off from a constituency of genuine radicals'.[56] This appealing to Blair has not so far done Livingstone any good. He has been blocked from standing as mayor on the grounds that it is better to weather an argument now and prevent him from winning such a prestigious position than allow him to win and then be faced with permanent opposition in London. Livingstone has repeatedly tried to assuage the Blairites' fears, most cravenly in a *Guardian* article where he offered to accept Blairite Trevor Philips as his deputy, to work with the government and to accept party control of the campaign.[57] This again received the predicted response and Livingstone has now launched a public campaign in favour of his candidacy for mayor, with backing from London Labour MP Diane Abbott, Billy Bragg, Jo Brand and other celebrities. A February meeting in London to launch his campaign attracted 1,000 people at short notice and during a tube strike. Even this campaign is described by Livingstone as 'aimed at changing the one vote that matters, which is Tony Blair's'.[58] The problem is that he reduces the idea of campaigning for a left wing candidate to one of manoeuvre, rather than basing it on rank and file support for the left wing policies which are marginalised under Blair. In addition, Livingstone is fairly typical of a new generation of left MPs who both reject the earlier radicalism of the hard left while presenting themselves as providing a slightly more left wing critique, especially of the economy, than Blair and Brown.[59] All this leads to a tacit acceptance of many of the fundamentals of Blairism and to a shared assumption that the old left is finished as a force and that compromise is the only way forward.

However, it would be wrong to deduce from the present weakness of the Labour left that it cannot regain its influence. Indeed, Blair's right wing politics open up a space for the left which can only grow as long as his policies continue on their present course. The Livingstone campaign in London is one obvious focus where it can grow, but will also do so around the issues facing Scottish and Welsh politics, around future industrial struggles, cuts campaigns and around a range of politics where discontent with Blair has come to the surface. In such situations, even a politically very weak left can suddenly find that it is attractive to large numbers of people looking for an alternative to Blairism. Already we can see that figures like Livingstone are supported because they are identified with a much more left wing politics than are currently on offer from mainstream Labour. Any big upsurge in struggle will see a much bigger audience for the left, and the Labour left will grow as a consequence. At the same time, its political compromises with Blairism, its organisational weakness and its lack of any real roots inside the working class, plus its lack of a coherent ideological voice, mean that it will find it more difficult to consolidate that support than has been the case in the past.

Those who expected a stronger opposition to Blair from the trade union leaders have been disappointed. In practice they have acquiesced to most of Blair's policies even though the unions have received very little in return for bankrolling much of the election campaign and for their loyal support for Labour. Despite spending £12 million in donations to Labour in 1996-1997 and providing 9,000 helpers in the election campaign, the unions have been shunned.[60] It is an open secret that the TUC leaders and the various heads of unions feel betrayed and outcast by Downing Street. Far from receiving favours from Labour, they are forced to stand by while the big bosses, many of them anti-union, have the ear of Tony Blair. On crucial union questions such as the minimum wage and the Fairness at Work legislation, agreement has been reached as a compromise between bosses and unions, only for Labour to renege on the deal and give into further lobbying from the bosses. Far from this leading to the unions taking a harder stand against Blair, it has made the leaders pathetically grateful for any crumbs they are given.[61]

Response to the attacks on unions as a body, especially the successive concessions to employers under the Fairness at Work legislation (even that title was abandoned when the bill was published) have been muted, with union leaders stressing positive aspects of the legislation such as slight improvements in maternity leave. Attacks on public sector pay are much disliked by the union leaders but they are terrified of leading a serious confrontation with the government. In fact, whatever the deep divisions between the Blairites in particular and the trade union leaders, the two need one another. The union leaders need a party from which they can win some concessions, however few or pathetic these might appear; in reality Blair is forced to rely on the unions for the block vote which has swung behind his changes time and again and for helping to sell Labour's policies to union members. The head of the GMB, John Edmonds, made a revealing comment about the relationship: 'Our 50 percent vote [at the party conference] is still a powerful weapon and no one should underestimate its usefulness to the leadership. We work out an unwritten code, if you like, that we underplay our power and that our first instinct is to support the leadership. We know the damage caused by divisions'.[62]

However, even the most docile trade union leaders feel themselves pushed to the limit by this government. They are constantly ignored or humiliated by those in positions of power. At the same time their members on the ground are increasingly restless. They make up a large proportion of Labour activists; during the 1997 election they were used to knock on doors to win votes for Blair; they have been left empty handed by this government. In addition, life at work is extremely hard, with pressure from employers over jobs and conditions. Public sector workers, having put up with years of Tory cuts, are finding no improvement and sometimes a worsening of conditions under the Labour government. Private sector workers feel increasingly insecure as the government refuses to intervene to stop employers from their worst excesses. No wonder that dissent is growing. Perhaps an interesting straw in the wind is a letter sent from Tony Dubbins, general secretary of the printers' GPMU union, to all the union's branches, which deals with requests from local Labour Parties for financial assistance in this year's Welsh, Scottish and European elections. Dated December, part of it reads:

> ...the union has been deeply involved in consultations with the party with the 'Fairness at Work' proposals, and we expect them to be published in the near future. It is our intention to hold a meeting of branch officers to discuss the proposals as soon as possible after their publication. To this end I am strongly recommending branches that they should make no financial contributions to the Labour Party for election purposes until such time as we see the shape of those proposals, and the branch officers' meeting has taken place.[63]

Similarly, anger in the Fire Brigades Union (FBU) has surfaced in proposed resolutions to the union's annual conference, several of which called for disaffiliation from Labour. Bedfordshire FBU demanded that 'the FBU immediately disaffiliates from the national Labour Party in reprisal for the betrayal by New Labour leaders of their union roots.' Tyne and Wear demanded a withdrawal of support for councillors on Labour controlled fire authorities 'who have been actively involved in campaigns to attack and erode conditions of service of FBU members'. From Mid and West Wales the resolution argued that 'the Labour Party no longer represents working class aspirations and has abandoned all pretences of being a socialist alternative...this union should withdraw its financial support for Labour until such time as it returns to its socialist ideals'.[64] While these resolutions have been ruled out of order because they require rule changes in the union, and so will not be debated at the conference, they indicate a level of protest at Labour's actions and a refusal to continue supporting the party uncritically. It is obvious that the discontent at shopfloor and bureaucratic level in the unions is growing and that, although Blair has relied and will continue to rely heavily on union support while pretending that he doesn't, the tensions are growing and may well erupt in unpredictable ways.

What is the alternative?

It is a major paradox that nearly two years into a Labour government there is widespread discontent with Blair and with New Labour but this is not matched by any rise in the level of struggle. The number of strikes is very low; even very obvious discontent such as that over nurses' and teachers' pay does not immediately result in industrial action. There appears to be little political opposition to Blair. Opinion polls show him with a high rating, there is little opposition within parliament, and very little that occurs outside parliament is reported. In the self referential world which New Labour inhabits, businessmen pay tribute to the government and it is still lauded by most of the people at the top of society. The right wing media might be turning against Blair, but there is so much about him that they admire that their criticism is still muted. Anyway, the Tory party is so deeply divided internally and so despised by millions throughout the country that few see a viable electoral alternative (apart from the nationalists in Scotland and Wales). It is therefore easy for Blair to pose as a one nation leader, to echo John Major in claiming that the vast majority are becoming middle class and that within a few years everyone who is now socially excluded will be able to climb the ladder of opportunity to an expanded middle class:

Slowly but surely the old establishment is being replaced by a new, larger, more meritocratic middle class...characterised by greater tolerance of difference, greater ambition to succeed, greater opportunities to earn a decent living. A middle class that will include millions of people who traditionally may see themselves as working class, but whose ambitions are far broader than those of their parents and grandparents.[65]

Yet the reality is exactly the other way round. Many groups who may have thought of themselves as middle class—such as teachers and nurses, bank clerks, even some college lecturers, are seeing their wages and conditions being pushed down towards the working class. The idea that they or their parents failed to become middle class because of lack of ambition is also wide of the mark. Most people are destined to do jobs which are relatively low paid, increasingly insecure and dominated by speed up, supervision and other features of traditional working class life. Many of these jobs are characterised by relatively high skills coupled with intense work and often long hours—exactly the formula which is supposed to transport workers into the middle class but which in practice still leaves millions in low paid routine work. No wonder that the majority of people see themselves as working class: in 1997 around 60 percent did so, whereas around 35 percent saw themselves as middle class. Despite the idea that society is becoming much more middle class and that the working class is shrinking, these attitudes have changed little over the past 30 years. The percentage categorising themselves as middle class rose only 5.5 percent between 1966 and 1997.[66]

Blair ascribes his election victory in 1997 to appealing to the professional and managerial middle classes. These are the sorts of people he goes out of his way to cultivate. But in reality his electoral success did not come from these people, but through winning the votes of groups who increasingly see themselves as routine workers, often white collar and skilled, often members of trade unions (whose overall decline among manual workers, as jobs in areas such as mining have disappeared, has been partly offset by a growth in white collar unions). Labour made particular advances among what are classified as C1s, who include low level supervisors and managers but are also made up of clerical workers. Whereas 47 percent of this group voted Labour (an increase of 19 percent), only 31 percent of ABs (managerial and professionals) did. This last group still composed the largest single area of support for the Tories at 42 percent.[67] This reinforces an Institute of Directors poll taken shortly before the election which showed that managers were intending to vote 40 percent Tory and only 25 percent Labour.[68] More detailed polls before the election showed that 60 percent of teachers intended to vote Labour and only about 15 percent Tory. This contrasted with 50 percent backing the Tories in 1979, compared with 32 percent for Labour. Similarly with nurses, a *Nursing Times* survey showed that 70 percent planned to vote Labour against only 16 percent Tory. Given that nurses and teachers are classified as AB groups 'the change in their votes alone would account for nearly half the growth in the Labour vote in this grouping'.[69]

Among Labour Party members there is apparently little support for Blairite or anti-working class policies. Majorities questioned in 1997 wanted more money in the NHS, less spent on defence, and some income and wealth distribution towards working people.[70] A recent MORI poll showed that approval of big business was at a 30 year low. Whereas in 1970, 53 percent agreed that the profits of large British companies helped make things better for everyone who buys their goods and services, by 1999 only 25 percent believed this, with 52 percent against—an almost total reversal.[71]

It is no wonder that within months discontent began to grow with the Blair government among its traditional supporters. Few could have predicted that this discontent would be sharpest among Labour activists and its traditional supporters in the unions. Yet this is what has happened. Much of the evidence is anecdotal, but it is widespread. In many parts of the country Labour activists have left the party or slumped into inactivity, usually through demoralisation at having to defend Blair's policies or at being taken for granted by a New Labour machine which assumes votes in strong Labour areas will always be there. This has been posed most acutely in Scotland and Wales, where the run up to the devolved elections has led to defections and disillusion. But that mood exists everywhere. A number of people have left over new policies: attacks on single parents and disability benefit; tuition fees for students; the bombing of Iraq. Letters in *The Guardian* repeatedly testify to the public renunciation of Labour. Some of those leaving are very much Old Labour but many must be some of the 140,000 who joined between 1994 and 1997. Labour Party membership has fallen over the past year. In one Liverpool council ward, where one of the three councillors is up for re-election in May and some fear losing to the Liberal Democrats, several constituency activists resigned over the bombing of the Gulf. Morale is low and activists are often not informed of public meetings held by their MP. Elsewhere in the city, in the Halewood ward, the branch chair resigned at Christmas over the bombing of Iraq. In Birkenhead ward meetings are very small and few are willing to take on responsibility.[72] In Bristol the chair of one Labour Party ward resigned after 15 years in the party. A former mayor of one West Country city has recently resigned from the party; in another town in Wiltshire the convenor of a factory is not standing again as a local Labour councillor. Bristol University Labour Students found themselves split over the bombing in the Gulf.[73] There are similar stories from around the country. A longstanding Labour Party member in Cheshire wrote an article for *Socialist Review* last December in which he argued:

> Blairism is conservative. It is also dishonest. Blairism won an election in the name of Labour, on the back of the two centuries of working class struggle that created the Labour movement and with the help and the subs of party members who believed they were getting a genuine Labour Party elected. Once in power it has revealed itself to be something quite different. Not just broken promises but the repudiation of the very soul and aspirations of the historic labour movement.[74]

Michael Knowles's conclusion was to leave Labour. He speaks for thousands who may or may not take the final step but who are so disillusioned that they are not motivated to go out and canvass, let alone enthuse about the government.

So Labour members who used to be active in most working class localities defending Labour policies, getting people to join, turning out the vote, are now often sitting on their hands. In south Wales there have been a number of meetings of Labour members around the contest for leadership and the Welsh Assembly. At all of them a sizeable number were interested in socialist ideas, were willing to buy socialist papers and so on. Labour's landslide in 1997 depended on the enthusiasm of Labour supporters to carry it through: 'A quarter of Labour voters reported [to MORI] that they encouraged others to support their party: only one-tenth of Conservative supporters did so, and whereas 12 percent of Labour supporters actively discouraged people from voting Conservative, only 3 percent of Conservatives took a similar anti-Labour stance'.[75] Blair has lost this enthusiastic support among many of his activists. There is also some evidence that newer Labour members who joined after Blair became leader are less active than older members; loss of support from the traditional activists is therefore a very serious problem for Blair.[76]

However, it is a much bigger problem for those who have traditionally looked to Labour and now feel betrayed. They have put up with repeated assaults on left wing policies, of accepting cuts and job losses in the name of achieving change, only to see their party run and influenced by some of the richest, least accountable people in British society. Blair has no feeling or empathy for their concerns and he is contemptuous of their values. The result is a crisis of Labourism as it has been constituted in Britain since the Second World War. Labour is not even committed to the very limited provision of public services and welfare that it was once. The process did not start with Blair, but with the 1970s Labour governments which back-tracked on commitments in the face of the first serious economic crisis since the war. But Blair has taken the project much further, with his open rejection of Labour values and his espousal of 19th century Liberalism. Many Labour members who have devoted their lives to political change through Labour see little alternative, but a growing number are realising that this is the end of the reform road. The cadre of the Labour left, especially the MPs such as Livingstone, are desperate to keep the activists inside the Labour Party, yet the more they compromise with Blair the harder it makes the creation of a left wing pole of attraction.

The defeats of the 1980s still mark the working class movement and still mean that employers are relatively confident, and organised workers often feel demoralised and unable to really bring about change. Blair has found better friends than he has deserved among the trade union leaders, who have repeatedly argued that nothing can be done to alter policy apart from quiet behind the scenes lobbying—which has been a total failure. His friends among former left wingers have also been invaluable in selling the various retreats over policy. However, while Labour members were willing to put up with a great deal to win a Labour government, there are fewer reserves of patience left, and even fewer reserves of loyalty to Blair. His failure to win the hearts and minds of Labour members in Wales and London is indicative of the shallowness of his support. So far, Labour has managed to keep the lid on opposition, but the nature of New Labour means there are few barometers to indicate the levels of discontent and the possibility of future explosions. These will also most certainly take Blair by surprise.

While the level of struggle has been much lower in Britain than in many other countries, there is no real evidence for British exceptionalism. The same mood of bitterness and anger which affects workers in Greece or Germany is also present here. The level of discontent is obviously growing, although the indications are still straws in the wind: the 500 workers from Brent who lobbied Downing Street over cuts; the public letters of resignation from Labour; the 82 percent vote for strike action against privatisation at UCLH and among Sheffield housing benefit workers; the sizeable demonstrations around Britain over the Gulf; the discontent exposed in union conferences; the protests over school and library closures; the joy at Peter Mandelson's departure. This is not simply confined to the Labour Party: many thousands are questioning the political and ideological assumptions which they have accepted for decades and are looking to a left alternative. Socialists are able to find an audience at two levels: through intervening in the small but important struggles against the ravages of the market and the compliance of Blairism, which are there even though they rarely make the headlines; and by providing some of the ideological arguments about the alternative to a society run in the interest of capital. It is increasingly obvious that even one major national strike or an all out strike in one city would lead to a rapid crisis of Blairism and Labourism as society polarised along class lines. But we do not need to sit passively waiting for such an event to occur. Instead we can begin to develop a theoretical and practical alternative to Labourism, old and new, which can point the way out of the chaos of the system.

Notes

1   *Marxism Today*, November/December 1998. See especially S Hall, 'The Great Moving Nowhere Show'.
2   See D Butler and D Kavanagh, *The British General Election of 1997* (Macmillan, 1997), p112.
3   See M White, 'Blair Hails Middle Class Revolution', *The Guardian*, 15 January 1999.
4   J Northcott, *Britain's Future* (Policy Studies Institute, University of Westminster, 1999), p59.
5   Ibid, p61.
6   Ibid, p48.
7   Ibid, p38.
8   Ibid, p41.
9   *The Economist*, 16 January 1999, p38.
10   J Northcott, op cit, pp133-137.
11   Ibid, p16.

12   D Butler and D Kavanagh, op cit, p57.
13   J Northcott, op cit, p80, demonstrates that the working hours of British workers are the longest in Europe, more than three hours longer than the EU average.
14   D Butler and D Kavanagh, p52.
15   Ibid, p109.
16   George Soros and Jeff Madrick, 'The International Crisis: An Interview', *New York Review of Books*, 14 January 1999.
17   See A Callinicos, 'World Capitalism at the Abyss', *International Socialism* 81 (Winter 1999), and R Hoveman, 'Japan Sinking Fast', *Socialist Review* 227, February 1999.
18   See, for example, the comparison of forecasts for UK growth during 1999 among supposed 'experts' which range from 2.1 percent to -0.5 percent in R Adams, 'The Difficulties of Long Range Economic "Whether" Forecasts', *Financial Times*, 3 February 1999. The author compared the forecasts to 'catching water in a sieve—not much good, but better than nothing.'
19   'Budget Games', *The Economist*, 30 January 1999, p35.
20   Ibid, p36.
21   'Private Welfare and Public Policy', Joseph Rowntree Foundation quoted in *The Economist*, 16 January 1999.
22   Quoted in S Driver and L Martell, *New Labour* (Polity, 1998), p29.
23   G Brown, *Fair is Efficient* (Fabian Society, 1994), p22.
24   See S Driver and L Martell, op cit, pp111-113.
25   S Driver and L Martell, op cit, p113.
26   At a seminar for academics and experts where everything turned on welfare recipients finding work, Gordon Brown was asked what would happen if he failed to get most people into jobs. He refused to contemplate this happening.
27   D Butler and D Kavanagh, op cit, pp313-314.
28   M Winstone, 'Spiked', *Red Pepper*, September 1998, p18.
29   C Bambery, 'Storms Over Scotland', *Socialist Review*, September 1998, pp16-17.
30   J Goss, 'Winds of Change in Wales', *Socialist Review*, July/August 1998, p9.
31   Quoted in S Driver and L Martell, op cit, p151.
32   Ibid, p152. See also A Parker, 'Lords Reformers Peer into the Abyss', *Financial Times*, 19 January 1999.
33   A Parker, 'Minister Calls for Voting Reform to be Scaled Back', *Financial Times*, 25 January 1999.
34   See, for example, M Linton and M Southcott, *Making Votes Count* (London, 1998).
35   Derek Draper quoted in the *New Statesman*, 10 July 1998, p10.
36   Tony Blair quoted in S Driver and L Martell, op cit, p26.
37   For a fascinating and graphic account of the interconnections see Paul Foot's Footnotes, *Private Eye*, 22 January 1999, p27. See also J Sopel, 'Profile of Derek Draper', *New Statesman*, 10 July 1998, p10.
38   D Butler and D Kavanagh, op cit, p295.
39   R Peston and G Parker, 'Negotiations Over Post-Election Pact With Labour Revealed', *Financial Times*, 22 January 1999.
40   R Harris, 'The Blair Project Sinks With Ashdown', *Sunday Times*, 24 January 1999.
41   Quoted in S Driver and L Martell, op cit, pp156-157.
42   T Cliff and D Gluckstein, *The Labour Party—a Marxist History* (London, 1988), p34.
43   Quoted in N Watt, 'Prescott Mocks Ashdown's Claims', *The Guardian*, 25 January 1999.
44   Quoted in N Watt, 'Blair Curbed Over Lib-Lab Links', *The Guardian*, 22 January 1999.

45   R Harris, *Sunday Times*, op cit.
46   G Parker, 'Ashdown Says Blair's Secret Ambition is to Split Labour', *Financial Times*, 4 February 1999.
47   G Elliott, *Labourism and the English Genius* (London, 1993), p60.
48   S Fielding, P Thompson and N Tiratsoo, *England Arise!* (Manchester, 1995), p106.
49   Ibid, p76.
50   G Elliott, op cit, p89.
51   Ibid, p66.
52   P Anderson and N Mann, *Safety First: The Making of New Labour* (Granta, 1997), p375.
53   R Adams, '"Dim Dawn" Primarolo Set to Dazzle Critics in her New Role', *Financial Times*, 27 January 1999.
54   Steve Richards' interview with Robin Cook, *New Statesman*, 13 November 1998.
55   D Butler and D Kavanagh, op cit, p207.
56   Steve Richards' interview with Ken Livingstone, *New Statesman*, 10 October 1997.
57   K Livingstone, 'I Only Want to Help', *The Guardian*, 29 January 1999.
58   C Reiss,'Ken's Challenge to Blair', London *Evening Standard*, 8 February 1999.
59   See, for example, the profile of Alan Simpson MP by John Lloyd,'In the Steps of Tony Benn', *New Statesman*, 5 December 1997.
60   L German,'A Landslide Country', *Socialist Review*, May 1997.
61   Steve Richards' interview with Bill Morris, *New Statesman*, 27 February 1998, and see the even more conciliatory approach a year later in K Brown, 'Meddlesome and Proud', *Financial Times*, 27 January 1999.
62   Steve Richards' interview with John Edmonds, *New Statesman*, 11 September 1998.
63   Letter from Tony Dubbins to all GPMU branches, circular No 255/98, 15 December 1998.
64   FBU circular 99 HOC 146 ML, 9 February 1999.
65   M White, 'Blair Hails Middle Class Revolution', *The Guardian*, 15 January 1999.
66   Ibid.
67   D Butler and D Kavanagh, op cit, p246.
68   Poll in the *The Observer*, 13 April 1997.
69   C Harman, 'Swing Shift', *Socialist Review*, June 1997.
70   Martin Smith's interview with Patrick Seyd, 'Whose Party Is It?', *Socialist Review*, July/August 1998.
71   K Brown, 'Approval of Big Business in Britain at 30 Year Low', *Financial Times*, 22 February 1999.
72   I am grateful to Suzanne Jeffrey for the information about Liverpool.
73   I am grateful to Mark Thomas for the information about Bristol.
74   M Knowles,'Why I Am Leaving the Labour Party', *Socialist Review*, December 1998.
75   D Butler and D Kavanagh, op cit, p238.
76   See interview with Patrick Seyd, *Socialist Review*, op cit.

TROTSKYISM
after Trotsky
The origins of the International Socialists

TONY CLIFF

After the Second World War, Trotsky's followers were faced with three dilemmas. Trotsky, murdered on Stalin's orders in 1940, had predicted that after the war the Soviet Union would be racked by political instability, that the West would be plunged into severe economic crisis and that national liberation in the Third World would only be brought to victory by the working class. Instead Stalin extended Russia's empire in Eastern Europe, the West entered the 'long boom' and national liberation movements came to power without the active intervention of the working class.

The state capitalist analysis of Russia, the analysis of the role of arms spending in sustaining the long boom and an explanation of the fate of Third World national liberation movements were the product of this attempt to understand the post-war world and its contradictions.

Cliff not only provides a brilliant introduction to these theories of the post-war world and their inter-relationship—he also explains why they continue to be of relevance to revolutionary socialists today.

BOOKMARKS PUBLICATION £4.50, AVAILABLE FROM BOOKMARKS, THE SOCIALIST BOOKSHOP
1 BLOOMSBURY STREET, LONDON WC1B 3QE
PHONE 0171 637 1848, FAX 0171 637 3616, email bookmarks_bookshop@compuserve.com

Reflating Keynes: a different view of the crisis

DAN ATKINSON and LARRY ELLIOTT

One disadvantage of writing for publications of the scope of *International Socialism* is the time gap between first thoughts and press time. Initial jottings for this article were made in January and made much of the 'eerie calm' that had descended on the world economy after the turbulence of last year. Thigh slapping self congratulation from the great and good concerning their brilliant handling of the crisis combined with an above average supply of gossip and trivia covering the Prince of Wales's girl-friend, the doings and sayings of dimwitted actors and actresses and the 'trial' of President Clinton to give the impression that the lowering thunderheads of 1998 were giving way to fluffy, benevolent white clouds.

But that was January and this isn't. Eerie calm has lost its old staying power and the crisis has re-emerged, bigger and badder than ever. The powers that be in the world economy are looking rather less like skilful pilots who have ridden the storm and rather more like the cartoon characters in *Scooby Doo*, who, older readers may remember, would laugh nervously at their foolishness at having been spooked by a floating net curtain or a prowling cat. Seconds later the real ghost would appear, moaning and gibbering. Britain today is like a haunted house waiting for the ghost. Overseas the phantoms are strutting their stuff and rattling their chains, and just about the only factor keeping them at bay is the vast, puffed up bubble of Wall Street. Messrs Blair, Brown, Greenspan *et al* are in an awkward position. Being modern thinking chaps, they don't believe in ghosts. Markets take care of themselves and government's job is an auxiliary one, supplying the corporate interest with a properly trained, properly priced people product and laying on 'supportive' legal structures and a sound currency. But the wailing and howling won't go away, so, half ashamed, they and their advisers seek handy hints by furtively thumbing the teach yourself exorcism book, in this case the works of the supposedly discredited old flake, John Maynard Keynes.

As the crisis deepens, we can also expect to see cigarette holders jammed between teeth and stout declarations that we have little to fear but fear itself as world leaders reach for the mantle of the original Keynesian statesman, the late President Roosevelt. But just as quoting a little dog Latin and waving a crucifix around is unlikely to make a non-believer into an effective exorcist, so affecting a jaunty air and tootling around in a wheelchair is unlikely to transform any of the current crop of premiers and presidents into a Rooseveltian giant.

When we began work on *The Age of Insecurity* in the summer of 1997, the disintegration of the Far Eastern 'Tiger' economies had only just begun. But the book would have taken much the same shape even had the Pacific Rim continued to enjoy apparently rude economic health. At the centre of our argument was a moral, not a practical, point. The loading of all risk and insecurity on to working people and the comcomitant 'age of security' for the financial interest was inherently objectionable in itself. True, the silent *coup d'état* by the free market interest in the mid-1970s had not exactly delivered spectacular results when set against the 'failed' post-war period of demand management and Keynesian expansion. Unemployment was higher, not lower. Growth was slower, not quicker. Real wages were stagnant or falling. Between 1990 and the end of 1996 one million people in Britain lost their homes as a result of mortgage company repossessions. Personal bankruptcies had 'stabilised' at 22,000 a year for England and Wales, three times the 'crisis' levels of the mid-1970s.

But a purely economic, quantitative analysis would have been little more than journalism in book form. Our view was that the malfunctions were traceable to a moral flaw in the free market system and that any analysis would have to start there. This explains the inadequacy and the ill fated nature of the measures currently being proposed on both sides of the Atlantic to fend off the gathering storm. They have no analytical base, and thus represent a series of unconnected, ill thought out, ad hoc responses from people who long ago triangulated and Third Way-ed out of their thinking any critical bent towards the market system. On this reading, all problems are temporary and government's first duty is not to make them worse. Furthermore, such problems are most likely have their roots not in the free market system but in 'barriers' to its proper operation—thus chancellor Gordon Brown's call last year for a World Financial Authority.

Would this body put banks and hedge funds under some sort of proper surveillance or control? Er, not exactly. It would be governments who would come under the beady eye of the WFA, which would be keen to ensure they did nothing to 'distort' the financial system. There are no free lifetime Mensa membership cards available in return for guessing who would be running such a body: secondees from the new breed of mega-banks such as Citicorp or Deutsche Bank and staff on loan from the International Monetary Fund, the international enforcement arm of the US Treasury.

A true Keynesian analysis would start from the belief that the free market, far from harnessing human moral imperfections to the public weal, amplifies and compounds them. A guilty secret lies at the heart of each stage of capitalist development, whether enclosures, slavery, colonialism or the appropriation of the law to deliver free gifts such as limited liability. In the words of Lord Hailsham, we do not believe the Old Adam has been banished by Adam Smith. No Keynesian would persist with the current fiction that treats giant entities such as Exxon or Ford as private economic actors indistinguishable from a corner shop or a one man carpentry business. By contrast, Third Way politicians behave as if such entities are doing their host nations an enormous favour by condescending to base themselves in the territories concerned and, unless they are treated properly, they will, at a moment's notice, up sticks and head off somewhere 'out there'.

But out where, exactly? Such corporations have no independent existence beyond that conferred on them by the law governing incorporation, contract and so forth. With no courts, no police, no bailiffs, no legal framework, they would crumple like a puppet whose strings have been cut. On the European continent there is at least some understanding of this. But the much trumpeted new era of social democracy in Europe is unlikely to be giving the financial interest many sleepless nights. Social democrats in France and Germany declare that the social model is not up for negotiation, that workers have rights, that *laissez faire* capitalism may be all very well for the Americans but not for Mother Europe and that, in short, mighty deeds are about to be done in defence of ordinary working people, deeds that have yet to be specified. In all the excitement it is easy to forget that all the tools with which Lionel Jospin, Oskar Lafontaine and the rest of the gang could have tackled big capital were surrendered by their predecessors. Europe as a bloc has foresworn exchange controls, signed the GATT free trade deal and pledged allegiance to the new economic system.

As a result, thousands are thrown out of work as bourses reel under a wave of takeovers and mergers. Belgium's banking system is dismembered, France is dragged into the era of 'shareholder value', and Germany's BMW ponders huge cuts while its rival, Daimler Benz, merges with Chrysler preparatory to massive redundancies. The not so bravehearts running European social democratic parties, confronted with the contradiction between lofty rhetoric and the reality on the ground, declare there to be no alternative, citing the 1982-1983 franc crisis as proof positive that monkeying around with the free market brings swift and severe punishment. Either Europe's social democrats are very stupid or very dishonest. The franc crisis did not 'prove' that domestic reflation 'doesn't work', but that domestic reflation is incompatible with holding a fixed exchange rate. Faced with the choice of abandoning the reflation or abandoning the European Monetary System, President Mitterrand and his finance minister Jacques Delors chose the former. At least they had that choice; both men then laboured mightily to ensure their successors would not, hence the hapless position of Mr Jospin in the face of chronic unemployment. To visit Brussels and talk to the European left is to enter a hallucinatory neverland in which all the problems of the world economy are more or less sorted out, with the euro sitting triumphant on top of the New Europe. In this Fantasy Island, Europe is menaced not by economic turbulence but by criticism of irrelevances such as 'enlargement' or 'the Europe of the regions'.

With European elections looming, it is worthwhile spending some time examining the attitudes of the British left in Europe to the international situation. Central to their viewpoint is the idea that world politics is—or ought to be—a mirror of world commerce. Hence 'multi-layered government' marks the way ahead, with a sort of global directorate keeping an eye on the big picture, regional head offices in Brussels, Washington, Tokyo and so forth and branches at national, regional and local level. Those who accuse Euro MPs in general of pursuing a secret agenda to shift authority to EU level miss the point; in the minds of Labour MEPs there is no ultimate focus of authority, merely a corporate style chain of decision making. All this suits the real corporations very well indeed, but it is hard to see how the toiling masses are supposed to benefit from the recasting of politics as a value free technical activity.

A leaked position paper on forthcoming talks on the Multilateral Agreement on Investment (MAI) makes the point. The MAI has been dubbed the 'multinationals' charter', with good reason; it would oblige sovereign states to remove all barriers to corporate activity, on pain of severe penalties. The EU is taking soundings on the MAI negotiations, and among those being consulted are so called NGOs—non-governmental organisations such as those dealing with the environment or Third World hunger. Hilariously, the EU has decided to treat 'business interest groups such as UNICE (the European federation of employers' organisations) or CEFIC (the branch organisation of chemical industry in the EU) as NGOs'. Therefore, roughly half of the NGO participants in the dialogue meeting were industry representatives, the other half representing citizens' organisations. And the viewpoint of these 'NGOs'? According to the EU, 'The European business community has made clear its position in favour of multilateral rules on investment both through its representative bodies (UNICE, ERT) and through informal direct contacts with investment decision makers.' There's a surprise.

But none of this seems of any great interest to the European left—or certainly not its British component—which prefers to fend off imaginary dangers such as a rerun of the First World War or the imminent introduction of death camps across the European Union. In conversation with the left's Euro-representatives, one is reminded of the story of the man who stood daily on a busy street in New York, waving his arms in the air. Asked by a policeman what he was doing, he replied that he was frightening away the elephants. 'There are no elephants in Manhattan,' replied the officer. 'Exactly,' the man said. 'Doing a good job, aren't I?' Key to their demoralisation, and that of their Westminster compatriots, is the conviction that technical developments have rendered their old beliefs redundant. Capital can move 'at the press of a button', they declare, thus 'old fashioned controls' are obsolete. This is the view summed up by Julian Le Grand of the London School of Economics on *Newsnight* on 20 October 1998. Attacking those who repeated the 'mantra' of exchange controls, he said Tony Blair did not think he could do much about globalisation 'and most thinkers think he's right'. Only non-thinkers, in other words, disagree with the world according to Blair.

Financial globalisation is nothing new: 100 years ago economists hailed the telegraph as having ushered in a single interest rate and a single world stock market, which it had, given the free market structure of that time. What changed the Victorian world market was not the tearing down of all telegraph poles but the political will to challenge the free market. The European left is very keen on political will as well, but sees it in crude quantitative terms: because corporations are big, political units have to be big to match them. This is the sort of economic and political illiteracy that, many years ago, reacted with outrage to the news that the pop singer Adam Faith earned more than the prime minister. It is the sort of size is important thinking that holds up the euro as a great hope for the left, on the grounds that it is (a) large and (b) susceptible, at some indeterminate future point, to manipulation by left of centre European governments in the interests of jobs and growth.

In such an atmosphere, the much vaunted, about to happen 'Euro-Keynesianism' is nothing of the sort, unless one simply equates Keynesianism with large public sector budgets and deficits, in which case the world's greatest Keynesian was former president Reagan. The basis of Keynesian thinking is law, ie the one thing the Euro-left considers to be politically unimportant. It is about the intelligent application of the law and the adaptation of the legal framework to right the wrongs of the market. It is, above all, a recognition that the economy is a human creation, not a force of nature, and that what has been created can be adapted.

Indeed, one true Keynesian of stature was not President Reagan but President Lincoln, who, in his 1865 monetary policy document submitted to the US Senate, declared:

> *Money is the creature of law, and the creation of the original issue of money should be maintained as the exclusive monopoly of national government... The wages of men should be recognised in the structure of and in the social order* [sic] *as more important than the wages of money... Money will cease to be the master and become the servant of humanity. Democracy will rise superior to the money power.*

This is all far too boring for the Euro-left, which is concerned only that Europe be a 'big player', able to call the shots in a leftish sort of way, in its dealings with big business. As if in guilt for having all but evacuated politics from their world view in favour of a conflict free vision of pragmatic deal making, the Euro-leftists make ritual calls for the European Parliament to be given more power, presumably so that it will be able to do more of nothing more effectively. When they are not hallucinating escape clauses into the Maastricht Treaty that may spare the continent from deflation and mass unemployment, they are congratulating themselves on achievements in which they played no part, such as the fall of the Berlin Wall. Sovereignty, the one legal status that has been proved to be capable of coming to grips with economic and social reform, is dismissed as a 'hang up' when it is not being condemned as the inevitable prelude to war, racism and genocide. Britain's Euro-leftists speak the truth when they deny trying to shift sovereignty to Brussels: they scarcely recognise the concept other than as a synonym for power or size. Presumably they take a similar view of the individual equivalent, the state of adulthood, and believe secretly (although they would never say it) that a poor or disabled individual is less of a person than a rich or muscular one.

It is common to hear European Labour described as a stronghold of Old Labourites. This is highly misleading. The left in Europe shares with Tony Blair the ability ascribed by John Laughland to President Mitterrand, that of shifting discussion to an area where no discussion is possible. Despite its deflationary credentials, the euro perfectly mirrors Euro-leftism. It treats exchange rates as barriers to trade, rather than facilitators of it. So do the Euro-leftists. It treats transaction costs as an intolerable burden, rather than an entirely natural feature of all economic activity, from walking to the corner shop to shipping oil from one side of the world to the other. So do they. Above all, it assumes that national currencies create differences, rather than reflect them. So do they.

In the Euro-left's euro fantasy, the euro currency zone will be a sea of tranquillity in which no bad things will happen. That the widely different economies of Europe will find expression for their differences through other financial instruments—as they doubtless will—is never considered. Only occasionally does the comforting idea that the big, big euro will biff George Soros on the nose come under any scrutiny. Yet success or failure in controlling capital is entirely a matter of political and legal determination and has nothing to do with the size of a currency area. Taking a dozen jellyfish and putting them together does not transform them into a hammerhead shark, merely into a very large jellyfish. But the spineless behaviour of the European Union in the face of the capital interest does not dishearten the Euro-left. Of course, there is plenty of reflationary activity in Europe but, in the absence of values, principles or politics, it expresses itself in the sort of Euro-Reaganism for which the continent's business interest is crying out. There is the Euroco defence and aerospace combine, planned supplier of taxpayer funded boondoggles such as the Eurofighter and the obsolete Airbus A3XX super-airliner to European industry. There are the trans-European railway networks, make work schemes for steel and engineering giants. There is Europol, to keep the populace under surveillance.

And there is the strained relationship with the United States, where policy makers are getting edgier and edgier about Wall Street's vertiginous rise as the Federal Reserve Board, the central bank, cuts interest rates again and again to keep the world system from toppling over. With even Microsoft's Bill Gates warning that new technology stocks are overvalued (the equivalent of Mr Coleman expressing concern at the amount of mustard being left on the sides of plates), Washington DC is accusing the rest of the world in general and Europe in particular of hitching a free lift on the back of what is—given the colossal borrowings and zero savings of US citizens—a hugely risky exercise in economic management. Some in Washington with a sense of history are doubtless recalling July 1927, when Benjamin Strong, governor of the New York Federal Reserve Bank, convened a confidential meeting of bankers at the home of Ogden Mills, under-secretary to the US Treasury. Also present were Montagu Norman, governor of the Bank of England, and Charles Rist, deputy head of the Bank of France. At issue was the need to maintain the boom of the 1920s. Strong had just slashed interest rates by half a point to 3 percent. He told Rist, 'I will give a little *coup de whiskey* to the stock market.' He certainly did that. The market surged ahead throughout 1928 and for some of 1929. By the time of the Wall Street Crash, Strong had died and was unable to defend what proved to be a reckless action. Almost none of Strong's additional liquidity found its way into productive investment. Instead it provided a reserve tank of petrol for the last crazy mile of high speed speculation. It all sounds horribly familiar, doesn't it?

Washington's anti-European strictures are given a special edge by the launch of the euro. The United States' pain-free deficit is built on the privileged position of the dollar which, as the medium for two thirds of world trade, is able to be a strong currency without being a hard currency. In other words, the US can borrow abroad without any effect upon the volume of purchasing power at home. The euro, despite its shaky start, threatens to challenge the dollar and bring the deficit structure crashing down. To talk publicly in such terms, however, would raise the intolerable threat of a genuine debate on the instability of the world system so, instead, Washington and Brussels confine themselves to arguments about banana quotas. Similarly, the White House, unable and unwilling to confront the real world crisis, manufactures substitute crises which it then 'solves' by firing missiles at Sudan and Afghanistan or by bombing Iraq. There was a special irony (probably not shared by Iraqi civilians) in the recent Iraqi air strikes, given that, on any measure, their legality and ethical basis are far shakier than those of the Kissinger-Nixon 'Menu' strikes against Cambodia in 1969, a series of bombings cherished by the Clinton generation as proof positive of Nixonian barbarity. Not even the North Vietnamese ever claimed the Menu raids resulted in a single civilian Cambodian death; today Blair and Clinton merely 'regret' the inevitable civilian casualties.

The hunt for scapegoats has become widespread as the crisis deepens, although it (usually) takes less life threatening forms. At home unemployed workers are told to look no further than the bathroom mirror in seeking the cause of their plight. They, through idleness, lack of training and a 'negative' attitude, are to blame. Around the world it is 'explained' that the latest scene to be visited by economic turmoil brought it upon itself. Thus Malaysia (pre-crisis) was the most exciting country on earth and post-crisis is a crony riddled, corrupt, one party state. Russia (pre-crisis) was vigorous, salty, bursting with rude energy, the new Klondike. Post-crisis it is a Mafia infested basket case, run by ex-Communists. Indeed, it has never properly emerged from Communism and is, in fact, still Communist, thus handily proving (once again) that Communism 'doesn't work'. Brazil, where the breakdown of its internal system of loans has brought the contagion to the American continent, ceases to be 'tomorrow's giant' and becomes an indolent nation full of Portuguese speaking layabouts who spend their whole time mugging each other and playing the guitar. This instant revisionism works both ways. President Clinton, formerly a discredited wide boy who wanted to nationalise the US health system, is now a far sighted statesman who wants to privatise the US pension system. Billionaire speculator George Soros reinvents himself as a thoughtful merchant philosopher, while even the sovereign state—formerly written off as a bit player in the exciting new borderless economy—is ushered in out of the cold and asked to propose initiatives to stave off collapse.

But in the absence of tough minded analysis, political leaders are more than likely to ask little or nothing in return for keeping the show on the road. This would be doubly mistaken. Firstly, it is simply wrong for the citizens of the countries concerned to write blank cheques, even were such action likely to restore calm. Secondly, it will not work. The turbulence of 1997-1999 is not some terrible aberration in an otherwise sound system—it is the system. This is how it is bound to function, with chronic instability, low growth, high unemployment and fragile real wages. Imagine a car without brakes. The only possible way to pilot such a vehicle would be very slowly, giving plenty of time to run to a halt when trouble threatened. Then imagine a salesman promoting the car on the grounds that brakes were unnatural, inefficient, an intolerable, totalitarian interference in the car's operation and, if applied constantly, the enemy of any kind of movement whatever. It is a truism that a car with brakes can actually be driven at much higher speeds than one without. It is also a fact that a brakeless car, even driven dead slowly, will still be involved in more accidents and worse accidents than one with brakes.

It is time to refit the world economy with some brakes before the current smash turns into a multi-vehicle pile up. There is not much time; as you read this, Wall Street may already be clattering and depression threatening. To end where we began, when writing ahead of events, it is always later than you think.

Explaining the crisis

NEWLY REPRINTED

A MARXIST APPROACH

Chris Harman

Since the early 1970s the world economy has been in a state of acute instability. Now the world seems to be facing the fourth and perhaps the most serious crisis so far. In the 1980s and early 1990s many proclaimed the triumph of the 'free market'. But the current crisis of the world economy has thrown their theories into disarray. Some critics have focussed on the anarchy of the financial markets. They have destabilised the world economy but there are deeper roots to the crisis of capitalism.

Crises have always been endemic to capitalism throughout its history. It was Marx who first provided a comprehensive and compelling analysis of the capitalist system, both in its periods of growth and boom and crises and recession. In this classic account of Marxist economics, Chris Harman explains the essential elements of Marx's analysis. He then goes on to apply those insights to an explanation of what has happened in the world economy over the century since Marx's death. Finally he demonstrates why Marx's central theories are superior to other analyses of the crises of the last 25 years.

Bookmarks publication £8.50 + £1.28 p&p, available from Bookmarks, I Bloomsbury Street, London WCIB 3QE. Phone 0171 637 1848, fax 0171 637 3616 email bookmarks_bookshop@compuserve.com

The new Keynesians: staking a hold on the system?

*A review of Will Hutton, **The Stakeholding Society** (Polity Press, 1999) £9.99*

PETER MORGAN

In the face of the recent crisis in the National Health Service Will Hutton made this one undeniable statement in his *Observer* column:

> *The harsh truth is that Britain spends too little on its health service. Another £1 billion a year over and above the increase in the Comprehensive Spending Review, together with scrapping the PFI, would allow nurses' pay to return to 85 percent of average earnings and new hospitals to increase rather than reduce capacity. This could be financed by...raising the top rate of tax to 50 percent for incomes over £100,000 a year.*[1]

It is articles such as this that have made Will Hutton a popular journalist. Throughout the 1990s, writing firstly for *The Guardian* and more recently with his weekly column as editor of *The Observer*, he has been a fierce critic of the Thatcherites and free marketeers who extol the virtues of unfettered capitalism. His best selling book *The State We're In* contained an impressive indictment of the Tories' market mania. And in this new collection of his writings, he carries on in this tradition.

Some of his most powerful articles are those in which he attacks the monetarist madness of the right wing, supporting his arguments with an impressive array of facts and figures. For example, in a *Guardian* article of July 1994 called 'An End to the Rule of Fish Market Economics' his attack was aimed at the new secretary of state for employment, Michael Portillo. At the time Portillo was keen to tell all who would listen that it was excessive pay demands of ordinary workers that were to blame for the high levels of unemployment and not the capitalist system. Quoting the results of a study by David Blanchflower and Andrew Oswald from their book *The Wage Curve*, Hutton drew a somewhat different conclusion:

> *Two economists have* [examined] *the data in twelve countries showing the actual relation between wages and unemployment—and what they have discovered will cause Mr Portillo and the free market acolytes at the Department of Employment heart failure. Free market theory would predict that low wages would be correlated with low local unemployment; and high wages with high local unemployment. But Blanchflower and Oswald have found precisely the opposite. In twelve countries the same law holds—the higher the wages, the lower local unemployment, and the lower the wages, the higher local unemployment. This is not a conclusion that can be squared with the free market textbook theories of how a competitive labour market should work.*[2]

But while the free marketeers of the Tory party are Hutton's favourite enemy, there is more to his writings than this, as the editor of this book points out: 'Will Hutton's political project [is] the creation and advocacy of a radical political economy that could both intellectually challenge the neo-liberal consensus and provide the fountainhead for a coherent policy package of progressive economic, political and social reform'.[3] Hutton, therefore, has styled himself as the person who can provide some answers to the problems that beset the British economy. Along with *The Guardian*'s Larry Elliott Dan Atkinson, Hutton helped to popularise Keynes's argument that the only way to stop the market wreaking havoc is for the state to intervene in the economy. In 1998 as the economies of Japan and the Far East lurched deep into recession, with the prospect that the crisis would embrace the rest of the world economy, the 'New Keynesians', as they became known, won new audiences. Under the headline 'Back By Popular Demand', Hutton asks, 'Is Keynes staging a comeback?' He then goes on to say, 'As our economies have become more marketised, growth has slowed and unemployment has risen. The search is on for a new theory and policy that might produce better results...[Keynes] offered a revolution in the way the capitalist economy should be conceptualised, and that should be the inspiration for revisiting his ideas'.[4]

However, whether Keynes's ideas can produce better results is by no means as certain as Hutton believes. Keynes was a critic of the free market orthodoxy. Under the impact of the 1929 Wall Street Crash he dealt a blow to the idea that capitalism was a self regulating system which would guarantee human happiness so long as it was left to its own devices. The free market argument rested on the assumption that capitalism would never go into recession, provided governments and trade unions did not interfere with its smooth running. Because the ability of people to buy goods is supposed to equal the supply of them, there could be no such thing as 'overproduction' where goods are unsold because people cannot afford them. It was also argued that there would only be unemployment if workers pushed wages too high for it to be profitable for bosses to employ them. It was an argument that made a revival with Thatcher in Britain and Reagan in the US during the 1980s.

Keynes pointed out that the supply and demand of goods did not necessarily balance. Simply because some people saved didn't necessarily mean others would borrow to invest—capitalists would only invest if they thought it would lead to higher profits in the future. Yet the fear of a coming recession leads more people to save and fewer capitalists to invest. Keynes described how capitalists, rather than being risk taking entrepreneurs, very often hold back from investing because they don't know what lies in store. So, he concluded, the free market inevitably produced unemployment and under-investment.

Keynes also attacked the idea that a cut in workers' wages was a way to restore profits. He showed how a cut in wages would lead to less demand for goods, more bankruptcy and even more unemployment.[5] Keynes thought governments should borrow money and spend to stimulate demand in the economy. In this way, he believed, governments were capable of preventing crises from breaking out. Crises exist, he argued, either because workers are not paid enough, or unemployment is too high, which means there is insufficient effective demand to absorb the goods produced. The result, therefore, is that goods remain unsold, profits are not realised, firms go bust and the economy goes into crisis. For Keynes the solution to the cyclical problem of boom and bust must be solved by creating effective demand.

Hutton is convinced that this strategy of state intervention could solve the problems of capitalism in general, and the long term problems of British capitalism in particular. Take, for example, his solution to the problems of the so called 'Tiger' economies today. Writing in *The Observer* on 23 November 1997 as a series of devaluations, stock market crashes, bank collapses and then IMF rescue packages hit the headlines, Hutton wrote:

The Japanese government first promised to respond to the prolonged slowdown in Japan by boosting demand; then it levied taxes; then it cut them—and all the time the banking system is plagued with bad debts and the economy by paucity of demand. What is required, simply, is an unconditional offer of international support for all Japanese banks—and a vast programme of public works to kick-start the economy. It may seem very Keynesian and very Old Labour; but anything less and the world faces the slump of its second biggest economy.[6]

There are two things to say about this. Firstly, just two years earlier Hutton praised the model of Japanese capitalism to the hilt as the system to follow, so some acknowledgement of a change in attitude might have been in order. In *The State We're In*, for example, Hutton wrote, 'If Japan maintains its current rate of investment as a proportion of national output, nearly a third as high again as the US, then it will be the largest economy in the world by 2005 while East Asia as a whole will become the dominant force in world output and trade by the first decade of the next century'.[7] In contrast, there were those on the left at the time who recognised that Japanese capitalism was in a deep and protracted crisis. Writing in *International Socialism* a few years ago Colin Sparks and Sue Cockerill said, 'Japan, for so long the wonder of the capitalist world, today displays many of the classic symptoms of economic, political and social crisis. The country of relentless growth is experiencing something that looks very much like the kind of economic stagnation familiar to other capitalist countries. There are few signs of any return to the years of boom'.[8]

Secondly, and more importantly, is the fact that old style Keynesianism is precisely the remedy that the Japanese government has pursued throughout the 1990s as the crisis kicked in—and yet the problems of the Japanese economy continue. Since 1991 the Japanese government has pumped $600 billion into the economy and cut interest rates to almost zero. Whilst these measures almost certainly stopped the slowdown getting worse, they have not lifted the economy out of recession, despite following Keynesian policies of fiscal reflation, cutting taxes and boosting government spending. In fact if we want to understand why the Japanese economy is in crisis, and why this has now spread to most of the world's capitalist economies, we have to look beyond the ideas of Keynes. Long before Keynes wrote, Karl Marx developed a theory of capitalism which showed that there were deep seated problems inherent in the system which drove it into crisis.

Marx argued that there was a tendency for the rate of profit to fall. As capitalism grows the rate of profit—or the rate of return capitalists get for their investment—tends to fall. The reason for this is competition, as capitalism is based upon the blind competition between competing firms. To stay ahead of their competitors, capitalists have to invest in new machinery to increase the productive capacity of their workforce in order to drive the price of their goods down and capture more of the market. But labour is the source of all value so as more investment is ploughed into machinery relative to workers being employed, this undercuts the very source of profit—and causes the overall rate of profit to fall. The growth in the ratio of capital investment to labour is not a problem for the individual firm—all they are concerned with is undercutting their immediate competitors. The problem arises for the capitalist class as a whole if every firm is introducing labour saving equipment. The greater the success of capitalists in accumulating, the greater is the pressure throughout the system for the rate of profit to fall. The most important reason why the world economy has faced such a period of prolonged crisis since the mid- 1970s has been because of the significantly lower rates of profit than that which prevailed in the preceding 25 years of the 'long boom'.

But on its own this does not explain why the system suddenly lurches into crisis—or why it is that the Japanese economy, for so long the envy of the capitalist world, is now in deep recession. So Marx also examined the cycle of boom and bust, more commonly called the trade cycle. Once again he argued that problems arose because of the competitive, unplanned nature of the capitalist system. While it is true that each individual firm may make investment decisions, the fact that the system as a whole is unplanned means that shortages build up sooner or later—for example in raw materials, machinery or labour. These shortages push up costs—causing inflation—but as the new goods come into the system from increased investment the market becomes flooded and the higher costs cannot be passed on. Profits are squeezed, certain firms go to the wall, there is a crisis of 'overproduction' (too many goods that cannot be sold for a profit) and the system goes into crisis. When the rate of profit falls it has an impact on the trade cycle, making booms shorter and weaker and slumps longer and deeper—thus producing the three recessions of 1974, 1980 and 1990. It is this process which underlies what has happened to the world economy in the last 18 months.

Marx did also argue that there were certain 'counteracting tendencies' which tended to push the rate of profit back up. The most important of these are crises themselves which wipe out large sections of capital allowing other sections to restore profitability and growth to resume. But that doesn't mean to say that crises are simply a painful but effective way for the system to rationalise itself before embarking on a new period of growth, because at the same time as crisis sets in there is a tendency for the centralisation and concentration of capital, in greater units. The greater the units of capital, the more difficult it becomes for a cyclical crisis to open up a new period of expansion, and the more catastrophic for the system a crisis becomes.

In the current economic crisis it has proved even more difficult for the world's ruling classes to restructure capital to eliminate excess capacity and overproduction. This is a point Colin Sparks makes about the crisis in Japan:

The way that capitalism would 'naturally' resolve such a situation is for the weaker capitalists to go under. Firms would go bust. Banks would fail...this has not happened this time round. The major capitalist economies are very reluctant to allow big units of capital located in their territorial patch to go bust...the prime example of this at the moment is Japan... Since the collapse of the 'bubble economy' at the end of the 1980s, it has proved very difficult to get the economy to grow [and] it has proved politically impossible to force through the restructuring of the large number of banks that have loans that are no longer making payments.[9]

Thus Marx provides an explanation for the crisis today but his ideas are noticeably absent from the writings of Will Hutton. Indeed in his two books, *The State We're In* and *The Stakeholding Society,* there are only three references to Marx—and these are cursory. In fact Hutton is even less willing to talk about radical solutions to the problems of capitalism than Keynes. For example, Keynes argued there was a 'declining efficiency of investment' which meant the system was prone to crisis which would ultimately get worse. The problem of how to get capitalists to invest for the common good of society led him to hint at far more radical solutions. At points in his work *The General Theory of Employment, Interest and Money*, which was published in 1936, he calls for the 'comprehensive socialisation of investment' as the means to secure full employment and overcome the worst aspects of the market. The answer then would be for the state to take investment decisions out of private hands. The logic of this analysis was too radical for Keynes and he never argued for it to be implemented. For the modern day Keynesians, such as Hutton, it is not even considered as it actually challenges the whole basis of capitalism—the accumulation of profit.

Hutton remains firmly convinced that the capitalist system remains the best way to organise society. So he says, 'It is true that competition and rivalry are essential to economic progress, markets produce winners and losers, and there is no economic system on earth that can spare loss-making firms from the pain of restructuring and redundancy. Profit is essential to a market economy and so is the freedom to trade'.[10] Whilst the revival of Keynes's ideas is proof of the depth of the crisis and the fact that many people are looking for solutions, by ignoring the most radical element of Keynes's analysis Hutton makes a massive concession to the ideas of monetarism.

The problem for Hutton is not capitalism as such, but the British form of capitalism. He remains firmly committed to the belief that the reason for the long term decline of British capitalism is that British society is dominated by a 'semi-feudal' state, which gives privileges to money capitalists of the City who are only interested in short term profits. Britain's interests, therefore, are not determined by the long term drive of industry for competitive investment, but short term profit making of financial institutions. In 'Money Before the Machines', an article written in *The Guardian* on 3 January 1995, he states, 'The heart of the problem is...a systematic failure of the financial system to commit to British companies—providing them with neither a stable, long-term ownership base nor with cheap long-term debt. Instead British finance is nearly always near the exit door, ready to bail out by calling in its short-term loans or selling its shares'.[11]

However, the British state is not a feudal relic, but was a product of the world's first bourgeois revolution. Britain has declined but not because it is not a republic, does not have an elected second chamber, or does not have a written constitution. Most of the great capitalist powers are as undemocratic as Britain. Indeed one of the most successful economies of the last 50 years until recently is Japan and this is headed by the most archaic form of rule—a feudal relic, the emperor. The fault lies with the capitalist organisation of society, not some British aberration caused by the domination of the City's pursuit of short term profits for the financial sector.

Hutton therefore has to confront the problem of short termism in the City and long term decline of the system. The solution, he firmly believes, lies with 'stakeholding'. It is a concept that remains remarkably vague, but essentially stakeholder capitalism comes down to persuading employers to act for the common good rather than for their own profits. For this to come about, Hutton argues, some form of constitutional reform is necessary: 'This is, in part, about recasting corporate law, and thus the legal obligations of companies to their stakeholders'.[12] Today the limits of constitutional change are being revealed as cosmetic tinkering with the House of Lords without any fundamental challenge to the root of the problem. Today's Blair government is much more persuaded and influenced by Robert Ayling, Bernie Ecclestone and Rupert Murdoch, none of whom will have their profits threatened by the constitutional change which Hutton is so keen on.

Hutton therefore ends up in the same camp as Blair. He never challenges the central contradiction of capitalism—the fact that employers derive their profits from the labour of workers. Instead he says, 'The [stakeholding] model has to be constructed around accountability and transparency, and operated by managers and workers alike who accept that they make common cause and have a mutuality of obligation'.[13] For many readers this may all sound vaguely familiar—it was the jargon of the 1970s and the Social Contract which ended in defeat for the unions and opened the door to the monetarists who became so dominant during the 1980s. Stakeholding therefore allows Hutton to make his peace with the market system: 'I accept that the price mechanism is the best means we have to allocate goods and resources, and that the signals of profit and loss are the most compelling means we can devise to drive both the level and composition of output in ways that correspond to real demands'.[14] Thus, despite his devastating critiques of the free marketeers, he can see no alternative to the market itself. He has opened the door to serious criticisms of New Labour, yet his vision of constitutional reform and stakeholding is entirely compatible with Blair's project. The capitalist system is so ill it requires a far more radical solution than either Keynes or his loyal disciples are prepared to advocate.

Notes

1   W Hutton, *The Observer*, 10 January 1999.
2   W Hutton, *The Stakeholding Society* (Oxford, 1999), pp16-17.
3   D Goldblatt, Editor's Note, in W Hutton, ibid.
4   Ibid, p31.
5   For a more detailed and comprehensive account of the ideas of Keynes, see C Harman, 'The Crisis in Bourgeois Economics', *International Socialism* 71 (1996), pp3-56
6   W Hutton, *The Stakeholding Society*, op cit, p217.
7   W Hutton, *The State We're In* (London, 1995), p269.
8   S Cockerill and C Sparks, 'Japan in Crisis', *International Socialism* 72 (1996), p27.
9   C Sparks, 'The Eye of the Storm', *International Socialism* 78 (1998), pp21-22.
10   W Hutton, *The Stakeholding Society*, op cit, p88.
11   Ibid, pp56-57.
12   Ibid, p272.
13   Ibid, p273.
14   Ibid, p1.

Brenner and crisis: a critique

A review of Robert Brenner, **The Economics of Global Turbulence: A Special Report on the World Economy 1950-98** *(New Left Review 229, May/June 1998), £8 paperback, £20 hardback*

ROB HOVEMAN

The mood prevailing among the world ruling class has swung between despair and euphoria since the July 1997 devaluation of the Thai baht began the current economic crisis. Until August 1998 the collapse of the Tiger economies was considered a local crisis that would ease inflationary pressures on the West. But after the devaluation of the rouble and the default on the Russian government's debts, Bill Clinton acknowledged that the world faced the most serious economic and financial crisis since the Second World War. Then the crisis seemed to pass and the ruling class breathed a sigh of relief. The financial markets recovered some of their nerve and began to chase the United States stock market up to ever dizzier levels. But just as they thought they were through the worst, the support operation for the Brazilian currency collapsed in the face of a further massive flight of capital out of the country. The financial markets, Western governments, central banks and the media have shown a schizophrenia which reveals the superficiality of their understanding of the dynamics of the economic system from which they benefit.

Robert Brenner's major history of the development of post-war Western capitalism, and particularly of the changing relationships between the three major Western economies, the US, West Germany (and later united Germany) and Japan, is therefore very timely.[1] In an analysis clearly influenced by Marxism, Brenner has sought to provide an analysis of the transition from the long boom through to the period of instability ('the long downturn' as he calls it) which set in at the end of the 1960s. He also outlines an explanation for why this period of instability has persisted for so long. Whilst his explanation for the transition is flawed and inadequate, there is much empirical detail from which anyone seeking to develop an understanding of the crisis of world capitalism will benefit.

Brenner's historical account

Brenner locates his explanation for the crisis ridden nature of the last 25 years in the fall of profitability in, above all, the manufacturing sector:

> *Between 1970 and 1990 the manufacturing rate of profit for the G7 economies* [the US, the UK, Canada, Germany, France, Italy and Japan] *taken together was, on average, 40 percent lower than between 1950 and 1970. In 1990 it remained about 27 percent below its level in 1973 and about 45 percent below its peak in 1965.*[2]

Brenner argues that the US (and to a lesser extent the UK) enjoyed a very considerable advantage over other advanced industrialised economies immediately after the war, both in productivity and productive capacity. West Germany and Japan had higher rates of capital accumulation but much lower productivity and productive capacity initially. However, their high rates of capital accumulation enabled them to begin to challenge the dominance of US capital in the world market by the 1960s, one indicator of which was a growing US balance of payments deficit.

The challenge posed by lower cost producers in West Germany and Japan to the higher cost producers in the US pushed down the rate of profit overall. As declining profitability heralded economic slowdown in the late 1960s and early 1970s, the US government sought to offset the pressure on US capital through a looser fiscal and monetary policy—ie bigger budget deficits and lower interest rates.

The post-war economic settlement amongst the Western economies was based on the Bretton Woods agreement which included pegging exchange rates to the value of the US dollar. It was intended that this exchange rate regime would provide stability for international trade and prevent the competitive devaluations of currencies which was one aspect of the great economic crisis of the 1930s. The chronic balance of payments deficit (excess of imports over exports) that emerged in the US in the 1960s, combined with the reflationary policies of lower interest rates and bigger budget deficits, undermined confidence in the dollar. In 1971 the dollar was devalued and the Bretton Woods agreement then collapsed altogether with exchange rates beginning to float against one another. The devaluation of the dollar put pressure on West German and Japanese exports as US exports became relatively cheaper and West German and Japanese exports relatively more expensive. The West German and Japanese governments then also sought to alleviate the pressure on their industries through more accommodating fiscal and monetary policies. The result was much higher inflation as the bosses took advantage of increased demand by raising prices rather than increasing investment and output. The oil price hike in early 1974 then pushed up inflation further.

Western governments sought to cap and push down inflation by raising interest rates and by trying to reduce their budget deficits, precipitating recession. After a weak stagflationary recovery in the second half of the 1970s, in which economic growth was almost stagnant whilst general price levels still rose significantly, a further recession, starting in 1979, was followed by the adoption of much less accommodating policies, particularly on the monetary side with higher real interest rates, the purpose of which was to bear down on inflation. This put pressure on US industry to restructure production to raise productivity and improve competitiveness.

In 1985 the Plaza Accord saw the US and Japan agree to push down the value of the dollar and push up the value of the yen to improve the relative competitiveness of US capital. Japan also adopted a loose monetary policy which deliberately produced the 'bubble economy', the rapid inflation of property and stock exchange prices at the end of the 1980s, the intention of which was to stimulate domestic consumption to help rectify Japan's chronic trade surplus with the US.

A further recession then followed in 1990 as the Japanese state sought to deflate the bubble which had got out of control (and the deregulated US financial system, which had been on a mad lending splurge, suffered a credit crunch—a fact not mentioned by Brenner who simply refers to the US suffering a 'cyclical downturn'). In the 1990s the profit rate of Japanese manufacturing failed to recover significantly and was further squeezed by the high value of the yen (until 1995 when it went into precipitous decline) and the general stagnation of the Japanese economy weighed down by the bad debt burden of the banks, which followed the bursting of the asset price bubble.

Brenner concludes his historic account (written in early 1998) by arguing that both the US manufacturing and non-manufacturing sectors had made very significant gains in profitability by 1996. This was the product of a rise in exploitation, significant restructuring of industry over the preceding decade, and the boost to exports from the devalued dollar. He speculates that US strength could be the basis of a worldwide recovery with increases in productivity and output not seen since the long post-war upturn. In addition he sees the possibility that the US's chief trading rivals, benefiting from the redundancies and restructuring brought about by the 1990s downturn, could provide cheaper goods for the US and world market, while soaking up ever greater quantities of US exports in a virtuous circle.

On the other hand, he believes it more probable that the attempt by the major industrialised countries to grow through an export led strategy whilst restricting their internal spending will lead to 'the perpetuation and exacerbation of longer term trends toward international over-capacity and overproduction',[3] a trend that is even more likely to develop in the wake of the South East Asian crisis.

Brenner's theory of crisis

There is little in Brenner's account to disagree with. The principal problems with Brenner's account lie in its theoretical framework and its distorting effect on his historical framework.

Brenner explains the fall in profitability in the late 1960s as a consequence of capitalist competition and the uneven development that characterises capitalism. As capitalism has developed, more and more capital has been sunk into enormous quantities of fixed capital, ie factories, machines etc. This rise in what Marx called the technical composition of capital, a trend visible over the history of capitalism, has been the result of a process of competition for markets in which every capitalist is under pressure to raise productivity and thereby lower their costs of production in order to compete more effectively. Unlike Marx, Brenner sees no problem arising for the rate of profit from this fact alone. Indeed, according to Brenner, rising productivity in the economy should imply both a rising mass of profit and a rising, not falling, rate of profit.

The problem comes, according to Brenner, when new, lower cost producers 'enter the line' and begin to compete for markets with the older, higher cost producers. Were investment in fixed capital relatively low, the higher cost firms could simply replace their old machines with new ones or else abandon that area of production. But in the real world of huge investments in machinery etc, such scrapping or 'exiting' is not feasible. Existing higher cost producers will rather seek to compete with the lower cost producers by lowering prices. They will suffer a reduction in their profits but will survive as long as they firstly, continue to make a profit on what Brenner calls their circulating capital, ie their purchases of labour, raw materials etc, and secondly, are able to cover their interest payments on loans that may still be outstanding on their investment in fixed capital. However, the consequence will be a reduced overall rate of profit for the economy as a whole provided the savings to the rest of the economy from lower cost production in this area do not accrue entirely to the profits of other companies using this lower cost production as inputs.

Higher cost production may survive for an extended period of time, Brenner contends, provided that relatively high cost businesses have access to credit which will allow them to increase investment and therefore competitiveness or just to hold on in the hope that the market will improve. 'But, precisely by facilitating the survival of low-profit firms...it [credit] tends to exacerbate over-capacity and over-production, and to slow the restoration of profitability, increasing instability and vulnerability to economic disruption'.[4]

Why does Brenner reject Marx's law of the tendency of the rate of profit to fall? His own theory would, after all, appear to be a distant cousin.[5] Brenner rejects profit squeeze/supply side theories which locate the decline in the rate of profit in the excessive growth or maintenance of wages and the declining growth of productivity due to worker resistance. Marx's theory too, according to Brenner, 'posits a decline in profitability as resulting from declining productivity'.[6] This is an extraordinary argument. Marx's theory is the exact opposite—the rate of profit falls because of measures taken by the capitalist class to increase productivity in order to compete more effectively against their rivals. 'The progressive tendency of the general rate of profit to fall is, therefore, just an expression peculiar to the capitalist mode of production of the progressive development of the social productivity of labour'.[7]

Competitive pressure forces capitalists to invest at least part of their profits back into improving productivity. Improving the productivity of the workforce enables bosses to cut the costs of production and thereby reap a larger profit by maintaining or expanding sales at the previously prevailing prices or by gaining additional market share and profit by undercutting less productive rivals. To raise productivity, more and more investment is put into plant and machinery and less into the employment of labour. So more and more sophisticated machines are introduced to displace labour. However, the exploitation of labour, paying workers less than the value of the goods they produce, is the source of surplus value, which in turn underpins profit. If more is being invested on constant capital or dead labour, as Marx called machines, and less on variable capital, the current workforce, then the rate of return on investment provided by the surplus value pumped out of the existing workforce will fall. What is rational and necessary for each capitalist to do in order to compete effectively has the consequence of undermining the rate of profit as a whole and thus creates the conditions for economic crisis.

Brenner ignores the labour theory of value and rejects the law of the tendency of the rate of profit to fall. His principal argument in doing so is to refer to the Okishio theorem. This purports to prove that any investment undertaken to improve productivity in the pursuit of higher profits will in fact lead to profits rising rather than falling. Indeed, capitalists would simply be acting irrationally to undertake investment that would lead to a lower rate of profit.

However, there have already been many convincing critiques of Okishio, most of which Brenner ignores.[8] The most compelling response to Okishio is that of course no capitalist invests to raise productivity in order to see his rate of profit fall. The first capitalist to improve his technology and displace labour in the process will indeed attract into his hands a bigger share of the pool of surplus value available, thereby seeing his profits increase at the expense of his rivals. However, the increased profit of the first innovator will decline as more and more of his competitors follow suit. Each will in turn attract more surplus value as they introduce the more productive technology, compared to the profit they were making when they were less competitive. That is why they are forced to improve their technology. The end result, however, will be that the overall rate of profit will decline for all capitals once the new technology is in place across the industry because less surplus value is being created by the direct producers, the workforce, relative to the total investment that has been made.

This tendency for the rate of profit to fall does not mean that there has been a continuous and inexorable decline in the rate of profit as capitalism has developed the forces of production, the technological capacity of the economy. Marx clearly argued that the tendency for the rate of profit to fall had to be understood in the context of a number of countervailing factors whose operation can prevent the rate of profit actually falling or help to restore the rate of profit after it has fallen and a crisis has set in. One such factor is increasing the exploitation of the working class in order to try to squeeze out more surplus value from the workers. If the rate of exploitation could be raised sufficiently, there would be no fall in the rate of profit. A second counter-tendency is the lowering of the costs of constant capital itself through a rise in the productivity in the production of machines, etc. A third counter-tendency is any systemic leakage of investment out of the circuit of the production of the means of production and consumption. Arms spending can be such a leak and had a stabilising effect on the post-war Western economies at least up until the late 1960s.

How effective these counter-tendencies are in sustaining higher rates of profit and for how long depends on the circumstances. In a recession it may become easier to raise the rate of exploitation as increased unemployment reduces workers' confidence to fight. Recessions may also lead to the devaluation and even destruction of capital. When companies go bankrupt, their factories and machinery may be sold off at 'fire sale' prices to be picked up by those who are still making profits. Moreover, competitive pressures may be eased and market share and profits boosted as rivals are forced out of business.

But there will also be profound problems in the countervailing tendencies smoothly restoring health to the system. For example, resistance from the working class will limit how far the increase in exploitation can be taken, and anyway there are finite physical limits to how long and hard workers can work and for how little reward. And as the units of capital become ever bigger, it becomes more and more difficult for businesses and the state to accept the clearout of the excess capital in the system, a clearout needed to raise profit rates significantly.

Brenner is right when he says that such is the scale of investment that companies will prefer to take lower profits than seek wholesale rationalisation and restructuring of their businesses. The growth of the credit markets has been important, as Brenner emphasises, in both stimulating spending and allowing big businesses in particular to weather the storm by increasing, rolling over (renewing) and even renegotiating their debts. Brenner brings out well how the financial system, underwritten by the state, has played a very significant role in propping up heavily invested business enterprises even at the cost of lower profits, ultimately, both for the businesses and for the banks. The alternative appears to be a potentially devastating collapse. Such a collapse might destroy enough capital to bring down the organic composition of capital and restore the rate of profit, but in the meantime many of the government's most fervent and closest supporters within the ruling class may suffer economic catastrophe and the seeds of social disorder and even insurgency may have been sown.

Brenner is also right that profits will be depressed by higher cost producers trying to compete with lower cost producers, rather than scrapping their higher cost plant. In effect their original investments are devalued by the introduction of lower cost technology by their competitors. This is a problem which in some areas of production, where technological innovation is occurring very rapidly, has worsened significantly. This devaluation might ultimately lower the organic composition but there will be no smooth transition here. Competition will be intensified and profitability undermined. Some sections of capital could take severe losses in the process, which in turn could precipitate severe crisis. This is all perfectly compatible with Brenner's theory and runs against Okishio's analysis, but Brenner's theory should be seen as a fragment of Marx's and makes better sense when integrated into the latter as we shall see below.

Brenner does not provide any new or compelling arguments to abandon Marx's theory of crisis in favour of his own theory, and his own theory has substantial weaknesses. Firstly, whilst it is true that older, higher cost businesses will lose out on profit to newer lower cost producers, why should this reduce the overall rate of profit rather than redistribute profit from the higher cost producers to the lower cost? Brenner's answer is this: 'Rather than merely replacing at the established price the output hitherto but no longer produced by a higher cost firm which has used up some of its means of production...real world cost-cutting firms, by virtue of their reduced costs, will reduce the price of their output and expand their output at the expense of the higher cost competitors, while still maintaining for themselves the established rate of profit'.[9]

This begs the question why the lower cost producers should only maintain the 'established rate of profit'. Brenner seems to be responding to this question in a footnote in which he says 'I assume here that the cost cutting firms compete amongst themselves, as well as with the higher cost firms, to drive down the rate of profit to its already established level.' But this will not do at all. Why should competition amongst the lower cost producers result in any particular rate of profit, as long as the rate of profit is higher than that of the higher cost producers? In other words, where does this 'already established level' come from? Brenner assumes that the rate of profit is established through competition but fails to explain what establishes one rate of profit rather than another.[10]

For Marxists there is an explanation for the rate of profit. The rate of profit certainly results from the process of competition but its level is determined by the amount of surplus value pumped out of the direct producers in relation to total investment on both machines and labour. The labour theory of value provides a quantitative explanation of what that rate of profit will be.[11]

Brenner also fails to explain why over time businesses cannot write down their older higher cost investments and then invest to update and restructure their production. There is after all some evidence of exactly this happening over the last ten to 15 years in the face of stiffer competition and a less supportive state and yet the world economy is even more unstable than at any time in the last 25 years. The fact is that despite this restructuring (and the increased exploitation that has gone along with it) profit levels remain well below the levels that prevailed during the long boom. The explanation for this is that effective competition at the international level in major areas of production requires a high organic composition of capital with the effect of continuing downward pressure on the overall rate of profit.

The profit squeeze theory

A major target of Brenner's account is the profit squeeze theory, which has been popular amongst some left economists over the last 25 years, and its cousin on the right, the supply side theory. These theories blame crises primarily on rising wages and falling productivity. Rising wages and falling productivity are themselves blamed on worker militancy and resistance to change. The policy prescription which follows from this profit squeeze/supply side analysis is for the ruling class to try to weaken trade union organisation to effect wage cuts, speed ups, redundancies and the rationalisation and restructuring of industry. Difficult though this might prove for the ruling class, if the profit squeeze theorists are right the contradictions of capitalism are not as fundamental as they would appear to be. It would not be unreasonable to assume that the last 25 years of sustained assaults on the working class ought to have restored the rate of profit to the levels of the 1950s and 1960s.

Brenner provides strong evidence in his historical account that the profit squeeze theory does not explain the onset of instability in the early 1970s or why this period of instability has continued for so long. However, his general theoretical arguments against profit squeeze theories seem to me less valid.

Brenner accepts that capital accumulation can produce a tight labour market (ie full employment or at least shortages of labour with the required skills) which will push up wages through competition between capitals to attract and retain labour and through the enhanced combativity of a more confident workforce. Excessive increases in wage costs cut into profits and falling profits then precipitate an economic downturn.

Other costs, however, are also pushed up as a boom develops. Bosses confident about expanding markets and rising profits increase investment. But that investment is unplanned overall and not co-ordinated to stay in line with the expansion of the supply of raw materials and machinery, as well as the supply of suitably skilled labour. Costs are pushed up, but when the new production from that investment comes on stream, again unplanned overall to match the likely demand for those goods, overproduction for the market pushes prices down. Higher costs that cannot then be passed on in higher prices squeeze profits. This is one of the explanations for at least some of the boom/bust cycles which have afflicted capitalism throughout its history.[12]

Brenner makes two arguments against this analysis. Firstly, he argues that whilst profit squeezes may explain local crises, they cannot explain the onset of generalised system-wide crisis.

Victories by labour in economic conflicts tend to be relatively localised; reductions in profitability resulting from the successful exertion of workers' power tend therefore to be correspondingly localised; nevertheless, there is a generalised, system-wide pressure on employers to make the average rate of profit on pain of extinction. To the extent therefore that workers' gains reduce their employers' rate of profit below the average, they undercut capital accumulation, creating the conditions, in the medium run, for their own eradication.[13]

Now it has to be said that for all one's sympathies with Brenner's ultimate objective, his arguments here are weak. He states as fact the inevitably localised nature of workers' confidence and militancy. This is not an absolute truth but rather a pessimistic picture of class struggle and the contagious effects of victory. But even given that there was considerable unevenness in the combativity of the working class as we moved into the economic downturn 25 years ago, Brenner ignores the fact that a generalised investment boom can cause shortages of labour in many countries thereby forcing wages up. Moreover the late 1960s and early 1970s did see a generalised rise in class struggle which did exert an upward pressure on wages. This did not cause the crisis—on the contrary, it was already existing pressures on profitability which led employers to mount the attacks which helped to spark these struggles— but it did reflect the effect of full employment on workers' strength and confidence, and it presented a major obstacle to capital's ability to overcome the crisis.

Brenner's argument against the profit squeeze theory also ignores the way other costs will also rise and cause difficulties for profitability as overproduction sets in. Just because some capitalists may benefit hugely from sudden price rises in the commodities they own does not mean that huge transfers of wealth within the capitalist class cannot have highly disruptive effects on the world economy. This, after all, is surely the lesson of the oil price hikes in 1974 and again in 1979.

Finally his argument ignores the transmission mechanisms that lead to a localised fall in profitability and therefore economic downturn in one country or region, transferring to other countries and regions and ultimately across the world economy as a whole. International trade will mean a fall off in exports to countries in recession, profits on investments in those countries by multinationals may also be hit and, as the financial contagion from South East Asia has confirmed, the financial effects of a downturn in one part of the world economy can have dramatic repercussions in other parts. How dramatic the effects of such a downturn in a national or regional economy are will depend on such factors as the relative size of the economy, the proportion of world trade it accounts for, international financial exposure to the economy and the general rate of profit prevailing across the world economy. Brenner's argument against profit squeeze theories of the onset of crisis therefore dismisses some of the elements needed to provide an analysis of the boom/bust cycle.

The real point here is not that profit squeeze theories do not have some validity in the analysis of crises, but rather why in certain circumstances downturns are relatively mild and capitalism can recover from them relatively quickly and in other circumstances they are much more severe and it is much more difficult to restore high levels of profitability and growth to the system. In other words we need a theory of longer term and more ineradicable trends in the capitalist system and a theory of the boom/bust trade cycle.

Here Brenner's principal argument against the supply siders has more relevance. His argument is that the long downturn could not have been so severe and continued for so long if the profit squeeze/supply side theories provide the principal explanation for the crisis of profitability over the last 25 years. Workers 'price themselves out of jobs', weakening confidence of other workers to resist speed up, wage cuts, etc. States vary in their ability to secure such increased exploitation but sooner or later will succeed. For example, there has, as Brenner argues, undoubtedly been a significant rise in the rate of exploitation in the US as wages have stagnated and even fallen from the early 1980s through to the last couple of years. Capitalists can also shift production, at least over the medium term, to parts of the country or to other countries where wage costs are lower and the workforce more 'flexible'.

Brenner's argument clearly has some cogency, but profit squeeze theorists might reasonably retort that such is the scale of investment in plant and machinery (a fact Brenner himself uses in articulating his own theory), and such are the links between particular capitals and particular states that productive capital is much less mobile even in the medium term than Brenner suggests. Indeed, this is an important argument against the wilder flights of imagination of theorists of 'globalisation'.[14] But if this is so, then the burden of reversing the decline in profits will fall solely on pushing down wages, downsizing workforces etc, within the social and historical constraints of the society in which the capital has been invested, and this could take much longer than Brenner allows for.

The problem here is that Brenner is again vulnerable to those statistical studies which have purported to show that the profit squeeze theory is correct. These studies have looked at national income statistics broken down in two ways: firstly to provide a picture of capital/output ratios (taken by some to represent the organic composition of capital) and secondly, the profit share (the distribution of income between labour and capital, taken as a measure of the rate of exploitation). Such studies claim that it is changes in the latter and not the former which are correlated with a decline in profit rates.[15] Brenner provides no serious challenge to them. Challenges do, however, exist in, for example, work by Fred Moseley, Anwar Shaikh and E Ahmet Tonak, and Tom Weisskopf.[16] The work of Moseley, and Shaikh and Tonak in particular, use the labour theory of value to recalculate the raw statistics that profit squeeze theorists content themselves with. This reinterpretation shows that the fall in the rate of profit in the US has been due largely to the rise in the organic composition of capital (and to the growth of unproductive, non-surplus value producing labour).

Arms spending and uneven development

Brenner accepts that arms spending had a stabilising effect on the US and the world economy for a period of time after the war.

> *During the second half of the [1950s], as the US economy lost steam...the hugely increased government spending of the post-war epoch—military spending in particular—was obviously critical for maintaining economic stability, not only within the US but in the world economy as a whole... During the 1950s approximately 10 percent of GNP went to military spending and, according to one major study of US industrial growth conducted in the latter part of the decade, 'military demand had been the major and almost exclusive dynamic growth factor in recent years.' Military production had a major advantage for existing capitals: its output did not compete for their markets.[17]*

It is a virtue of Brenner's argument here that he sees arms spending not only as a Keynesian style demand boost to the economy, counteracting declines in the rate of private capital accumulation, but also as having a special role to play in alleviating downward pressures on the rate of profit arising out of the process of competitive accumulation itself, because armaments are not in general thrown back onto the market.

However, the analysis would be strengthened in two ways if he were to accept the analysis established by Cliff, Kidron and Harman. Firstly, arms spending offset the tendency of the rate of profit to fall in the long boom because it represented a diversion of investment away from the production of the means of production and of consumption. Arms spending failed to feed back into the productive circuit of capital. It therefore did not depress the rate of profit by raising the organic composition of capital.

Secondly, although Brenner is right to see that the erosion of US competitiveness by German and Japanese capital put downward pressure on the rate of profit, he ignores the fact that the concentration of arms spending in the US and the UK allowed Germany and Japan, limited in their arms investment as a result of the post-war settlement, to gain that competitive advantage which in turn forced the US and UK to reduce arms investment. This fits so neatly into Brenner's uneven development account of the crisis that it is surprising he does not see its pertinence.

The fall in arms spending did release funds for productive investment, encouraged by the need of US and UK capital to fight off German and Japanese competition. And this began to push down the rate of profit as the organic composition of capital began to rise on a world scale.

The great strength of the theory of the permanent arms economy was that it provided a theory of why capitalism had entered the long boom and also identified why that long boom could not persist forever. It is a theory that was crucially connected to a certain view of how the concentration and centralisation of capital had changed the role of the state, ushering in an era of state capitalism in which economic competition was increasingly accompanied and even displaced by military competition. This change in the nature of world capitalism in the 20th century provides an explanation for the two massively destructive world wars and the unprecedented levels of peacetime arms spending that took place during the Cold War.[18]

Brenner does not provide any of this framework and, although he has an analysis of why the long boom came to an end, there is no indication in his general theory, or his empirical description, of how the theory of crisis would apply in different periods. For example, is the Great Depression of the 1930s explicable in terms of Brenner's theory and if so how did capitalism get out of it and bring about the long boom? And what of the crises of the 19th century?

The state and internationalisation

Brenner's historical account concentrates on three blocs of capital, the US, West Germany and Japan, and their interrelations. He does not provide a broader theorisation of the changing relationship of capital and state and fails to theorise the growing internationalisation of trade, production and finance.[19] This internationalisation has meant greater limits being placed on individual states' room for manoeuvre; limits on the ability to reflate the economy, to manipulate its exchange rate and to control its interest rates. This is not to say that states have lost all power and we now live in a completely laissez faire world. However, Brenner's account excessively concentrates on the three blocs as though they constituted cohesive units of capital, where states have relative freedom of action in relation to the other blocs.

Brenner's failure to theorise these complex and contradictory relationships is most in evidence in his failure to give an adequate account of the growth and the internationalisation of the financial system. Naturally, we should not fall into the illusion that the travails of world capitalism are the product of an ideologically driven deregulation of the financial system which has turned world capitalism into a casino. We are on Brenner's side in emphasising how the fall in the rate of profit in the productive sector has been fundamental to the instability of the last 25 years. However, the financial system is an integral part of any capitalist system and developments in recent years have brought into existence far greater forces of instability. Although Brenner makes limited reference to the financial system, particularly in relation to exchange rates between the three major blocs, his account suffers from analysing exchange rates only in terms of state management. More fundamentally, he does not provide an adequate explanation of the globalisation of financial capital and the implications of it for the instability of world capitalism. No analysis of the current crisis can afford to omit an account of the destabilising effects of the international financial system, of the power of the state to prop the system up and the limits on that power posed by internationalisation and deregulation.[20]

Brenner's conclusion

Finishing his account in early 1998, Brenner left open the question of whether there would be a new boom or the continuation of the instability brought on by overproduction and overcapacity and the attendant depressed profit rates. In his 'optimistic' scenario of a new boom Brenner ends up by implying that, now the US has restructured so successfully, there may be sunny uplands ahead if only major states abandoned policies which were depressing domestic spending, originally necessary to effect restructuring, and now adopted more expansionary policies to boost domestic consumption. Such policies could produce once again a virtuous circle of higher profits and higher growth.

But this is the most naive Keynesianism which ignores the ongoing contradictions in the process of competition and the production of an adequate rate of profit. Firstly, Brenner exaggerates the recovery of profitability in the US. Joel Geier and Ahmed Shawki have demonstrated that profit rates in manufacturing industry in the US in the 1990s have only risen to levels comparable to those prevailing just before the onset of the serious recession of 1974.[21]

Secondly, he provides little evidence that the unevenness in the development of capitalist productivity, which is at the heart of his theory of crisis, has in any way diminished in the last few years. There would appear to have been significant shifts in the balance of advantage between Japan, Germany and the US over the last few years, but Brenner provides no evidence that this has diminished the imbalance between higher and lower cost producers which he believes is the primary cause of lower profit rates. Brenner may have been misled here by his excessively nationally oriented analysis. Even though the balance of advantage may have shifted between national economies and may have changed on an aggregate basis, this does not mean that in particular industries both within and between countries, the imbalance between higher and lower cost producers does not persist. Difference in investment rates constantly renew such imbalances. Japan's rate of productive investment in export oriented industries has held up at relatively high rates at least until the last couple of years. And the enormous investment boom in South East Asia in the 1990s, only some of which spilled over into speculation, has meant a very significant growth of lower cost production in areas of internationally tradable goods, putting pressure on the profitability of producers in the advanced industrialised countries. Moreover, the speed with which costs have fallen in particular industries in recent years as a result of technological innovation can give even greater advantages to 'late' entry producers.

Brenner fails to identify a further element which should counter the idea that any such uplands are around the corner. The US may have had some success in both restructuring capital to raise productivity and the pressures of recession and stagnation in the German and Japanese economies may have produced some similar if even more limited successes there. We should therefore avoid the idea that world capitalism is simply stuck in stagnation as states seek to avoid the potentially cataclysmic consequences of clearing out the excess capital which is holding profit rates down. Capitalism is not a static system. The instability of the last 25 years has been a history of sharp crises and recessions followed by some recovery in growth and profit rates.

Those recoveries have, however, been limited and contradictory demonstrating the limited success the ruling class has had in restoring profit rates on a sustainable basis. Moreover, the revival of investment in the last three or four years in the US, the high levels of productive investment in Japan even up until 1996, despite domestic stagnation and an incipient banking crisis, and the very high levels of productive investment in the Tigers at least until their collapse, are all indicators of strong potential upward pressure on the organic composition of capital worldwide, and therefore downward pressure on the rate of profit, despite higher rates of exploitation and restructuring.[22]

With profit rates still relatively low worldwide, with financial markets continuing to show high levels of volatility, which lower interest rates may not be sufficient, in the short term anyway, to counter, the prospects are not for a new boom but rather for an unfolding crisis which it will be very difficult for the ruling class to contain. This conclusion, which was foreshadowed in this journal in spring 1998[23] and which has grown out of Marx's theory of crisis applied to the contemporary world, seems much closer to the mark than Brenner's.

The labour theory of value is fundamental in identifying that exploitation is the source of profit in the system, that there is a fundamental conflict of interest between the capital and labour and in providing the framework in which Marx's law of the tendency of the rate of profit to fall makes sense. And the falling rate of profit theory is vital in understanding why crises occur under capitalism, why they have become so intractable and why there is no alternative to the needless destruction and barbarism of capitalism short of socialism—a socialism in which those who produce the wealth in society, the working class, collectively plan that production to meet need rather than profit.

Notes

1   Brenner has given his name to a major debate on the left over the transition from feudalism to capitalism. His analysis of that transition focused on the class struggle to the detriment of an acknowledgement of the key role played by the gradual development of the forces of production which, when fettered by the relations of production, generated the era of revolution out of which capitalism finally emerged. For a clear exposition and convincing critique of Brenner's position on the transition from feudalism to capitalism, see C Harman, *Marxism and History* (London, 1998), ch1.

2   R Brenner, *New Left Review* 229, May/June 1998, p7.

3   Ibid, p261.

4   Ibid, p34.

5   Brenner, in fact, absurdly suggests that Marx's theory shares a Malthusian character with the profit squeeze/supply side theories to which he is strongly opposed. Malthus argued that economic crisis was the product of the tendency of the population to grow more quickly than any improvement in the productivity of agriculture. The connection between Malthus and profit squeeze/supply side theories is that the latter argue that in certain conditions productivity growth will fail to keep pace with wage growth thereby cutting profits. In other words economic crisis is the result of a 'secular tendency to the declining growth of labour productivity.' Ibid, p10.

6   R Brenner, op cit, p11.

7   K Marx, *Capital*, vol 3, ch 13 (London, 1981), p213.

8   Responses to Okishio are to be found, for example, in C Harman, *Explaining the Crisis* (London, 1983), ch 1; J Weeks, *Capital and Exploitation* (London, 1981), ch 8; J Weeks, 'Equilibrium, Uneven Development and the Tendency of the Rate of Profit to Fall', *Capital and Class* 16 (1982); P N Junankar, *Marx's Economics* (Oxford, 1982), pp99-101; D Foley, *Understanding Capital* (Cambridge, 1986), pp136-139; G Carchedi, *Frontiers of Political Economy* (London, 1991), pp140-141; and E Mandel and A Freeman (eds), *Ricardo, Marx and Sraffa* (London, 1984), passim. Foley has demonstrated that Okishio's theorem is only valid on the assumption that the real wage (the basket of consumption goods that a worker can afford to buy) remains constant. This in turn implies that all of the benefits of an increase in the productivity of labour will accrue to the capitalist class. A much

more realistic assumption would be that some of the benefits of higher productivity will accrue to the working class in the form of higher living standards, ie a higher real wage. This is, of course, perfectly compatible with a fall in the value of labour power and a rising rate of exploitation, as Marx pointed out.

9   R Brenner, op cit, p25.
10   In this he seems to be rather perversely following Adam Smith's theory of profit.
11   To put the point algebraically, let the value of constant capital (machines etc) = c, the value of variable capital (labour) = v and surplus value (the basis of profit) = s. The organic composition of capital is represented by the ratio of constant capital to variable capital, c/v. A rising organic composition of capital therefore occurs when c increases relative to v. The rate of profit is defined as the return on the whole of the capital invested. The return may be equated to the surplus value that is produced and realised. The total investment is equivalent to the sum of the constant capital and variable capital. The rate of profit is therefore given by $s/c + v$. The rate of exploitation is defined as the ratio of surplus value to the variable capital (wages) or s/v. If c rises more quickly relative to v, which it is likely to do in the pursuit of competitive advantage from higher productivity, then the rate of profit $s/c + v$ will fall unless s increases significantly as a result of increased exploitation.
12   It is worth noting that, in the model of the business cycle Marx develops in *Capital*, vol 1, pt 7 (London, 1976), he makes fluctuations in wages an important determinant of overall fluctuations in the economy, and in *Capital*, vol 3 (London, 1981), he dismisses the underconsumptionist theory of crisis pointing out that wages tend to rise at the peak of the cycle. I owe these points to Alex Callinicos.
13   R Brenner, op cit, p21.
14   See in particular C Harman, 'Globalisation: a Critique of a New Orthodoxy', *International Socialism* 73 (1996).
15   Studies of this kind include A Glyn and B Sutcliffe, *British Capitalism, Workers and the Profit Squeeze* (London, 1972); A Glyn, J Harrison and P Armstrong, *World Capitalism Since 1945* (London, 1991); and T Weisskopf, 'Marxian Crisis Theory and the Rate of Profit in the Post-War US Economy', *Cambridge Journal of Economics*, 3(1), March 1979.
16   See F Moseley, *The Falling Rate of Profit in the Post-War United States Economy* (London, 1991); A Shaikh and E A Tonak, *Measuring the Wealth of Nations* (Cambridge, 1994); and T Weisskopf, 'A Comparative Analysis of Profitability Trends in the Advanced Capitalist Economies', in F Moseley and E Wolff, *International Perspectives on Profitability and Accumulation* (Aldershot, 1992).
17   R Brenner, op cit, p56. Brenner refers to R DeGrasse, *Military Expansion, Economic Decline* (New York, 1983), pp20-21; and S H Robock, *Changing Regional Economies* (Midwest Research Institute, 1957); MRI-252, quoted in M Wiedenbaum, 'Some Economic Aspects of Military Procurement', *Current Economic Comment* (November 1960), p10. He ignores the extensive literature on the effects of the permanent arms economy in, for example, M Kidron, *Western Capitalism Since the War* (London, 1970), and C Harman, *Explaining the Crisis* (London, 1984).
18   The pioneering analysis of the permanent arms economy is to be found in T Cliff, 'Perspectives for the Permanent War Economy' in *Neither Washington Nor Moscow* (London, 1982), pp101-107. It was then developed by M Kidron in *Western Capitalism since the War*, op cit, and C Harman in *Explaining the Crisis*, op cit. The relevance of the theory of state capitalism, first established in relation to Russia in T Cliff, *State Capitalism in Russia* (London, 1988), is demonstrated in T Cliff, *Trotskyism after Trotsky* (London, 1999), and in many other writings including C Harman, *Explaining the Crisis*, op cit, and 'The State and Capitalism Today', *International Socialism* 51 (1991).

19   See C Harman, ibid.
20   For more on this see R Hoveman, 'Financial Crises and the Real Economy', *International Socialism* 78 (1998), pp55-76.
21   See J Geier and A Shawki, 'Contradictions of the "Miracle" Economy', *International Socialist Review* 2, Fall 1997, p7.
22   I may be accused of making *a priori* assumptions here myself. In response I would say that, if one accepts the cogency of Marx's theory of crisis, then intensified worldwide competition and the reinvestment this will force should, other things being equal, raise the organic competition of capital and push down the rate of profit. However, to prove that other things have been equal, detailed empirical work and analysis is much needed.
23   See *International Socialism* 78, 79 and 81 (all 1998).

Art and alienation: a reply to John Molyneux

CHRIS NINEHAM

John Molyneux's article in *International Socialism* 80 is of course right to defend the validity of modern art against anyone who rejects it outright as a fraud or condemns it all for being unrealistic. Marxists have always taken maximum freedom of expression as a precondition for authentic art. In Trotsky's words, 'Art, like science, not only does not seek orders, but by its very essence cannot tolerate them'.[1] But as well as preserving a fierce defence of freedom of expression we should not lose the habit of lively criticism and discrimination in the arts. The problem is that in his haste to take on right wingers like Roger Scruton who oppose anything modern by instinct, John ends up presenting a one sided analysis of art in capitalist society. In the process his defence throws up some arguments which have doubtful implications for Marxist theory.

To start with John overstates the level of mainstream hostility to contemporary art. He says much, if not all, modern art 'is regarded as a dubious or perhaps downright fraudulent activity by a substantial proportion of at least four groups of people'.[2] Judging by media coverage of the arts, the massive expansion of the art market, and the figures he himself gives for exhibition attendances, I suspect modern art is all the rage among at least one his groups, 'the educated/cultural middle class', and hardly controversial in another, 'the philistine bourgeoisie proper'. Even the media's attitude has changed dramatically from the days of scoffing at 'the bricks in the Tate'. John's judgement here is not accidental; for him art is fundamentally counterposed to capitalism. In his conclusion he says his argument leaves socialists 'defending art for its rebelliousness, its creativity and human values, while recognising that art as a privileged sphere of these qualities is the other side of the coin of a society which denies the vast majority creativity and humanity in their daily work and lives'.[3] Surely our job is a bit more complicated. Isn't the fact that art exists in this 'privileged sphere', separated from the life and concerns of the vast majority, going to have some fairly devastating effects on the art itself? And doesn't this have implications for our attitude to art?

At the heart of John's argument is the contention that art can be defined as unalienated labour. For Marxists, the root of alienation lies in capitalist exploitation, in the fact that the capitalist owns the means of production in society and runs production for profit. Labour becomes a means to create maximum profit by maximising output. In the process the worker loses control over the finished product and the nature of the product itself is determined by the dictates of the market; 'the external character of labour for the worker appears in the fact that it is not his own, but someone else's, that it does not belong to him, that in it he belongs, not to himself, but to another'.[4]

The worker ceases to recognise himself in the product of his labour; 'he is related to the product of his labour as to an alien object'.[5] Worse still, by losing control over his own labour the worker is separated from his own essential powers; 'How could the product of the workers' activity confront him as something alien if it were not for the fact that in the act of production he was estranging himself from himself?'[6]

It seems rash to suggest that artistic production is in a simple way immune from such powerful processes. Marx certainly didn't think so. He argued that 'capitalist production is hostile to certain branches of production, in particular, art and poetry' and 'the bourgeoisie has stripped of its halo every occupation hitherto honoured and looked up to with reverent awe. It has converted the physician, the lawyer, the priest, the poet, the man of science, into its paid wage labourers'.[7]

In early capitalism, art was regarded as distinct from commercial production. Adam Smith, for example, regarded artistic labour as unproductive from an economic point of view.[8] Indeed, it was only under emerging capitalism that art began to be considered as something separate from the craftsmanship associated with religious institutions or the court. But with the spread of commodity production into every nook and cranny of social life, a straightforward distinction between commercial and artistic production becomes extremely difficult. John's definition of art as unalienated labour runs the risk of favouring in advance the work of the individual fine artist in their garret who appears to control their productive activity over the collective work of musicians, technicians,

actors and so on who produce in the undeniably commercial and therefore alienated fields of film, architecture or popular music. He counters
this objection by arguing that, in cases of artistic acheivement in such
spheres, 'what makes them art is the non-alienated labour contributed by
directors, composers, soloists, designers, architects, etc'.[9] Apart from
being a rather circular argument, as well as potentially elitist, this begs
the question whether non-alienated labour in John's usage is a spiritual
concept, a state of being true to oneself, or an actual description of a relationship to the means of production.

Either way, I would argue that this uncertainty points to a more complicated and shifting relationship between capitalism and artistic
production than John's basic position suggests. As capitalism has developed, the social role of artists has changed. Commodification of art has
shaped artistic production itself and, far from being immune from it,
artists have grappled with alienation since the middle of the 19th century
at least.

The Marxist cultural historian Ernst Fischer argues that 'artists in pre-
capitalist societies were on the whole integrated with the social body to
which they belonged'.[10] In the early bourgeois period artists were still
valued for the ideological and spiritual weight they could bring to an
emerging class. The proud subjectivity of the artist neatly tallied with the
ideology of the bourgeoisie; the unification of the country and of
humanity in the spirit of liberty, equality and fraternity. The French
painter David, for example, was not only the official painter of the
French Revolution of 1789, designing festival sets, painting posters and
recording scenes from the revolution, he was also active as a legal expert
and as a politician in his own right.

During the 19th century this organic relationship between the most
advanced artists and the bourgeoisie began to break down. The promises
of the bourgeois revolution were being betrayed. From Goya in Spain to
Beethoven in Vienna, artists expressed bitter disillusion with the high
handedness and cynicism of the Napoleonic armies. In France many
artists took to the barricades against the government during the revolutions of 1830 and 1848. By the second half of the century the official
artists of the academy were churning out empty sentimentalisations of
rural life and cringing portraits of government officials in pseudo-
classical get up. Courbet, the great mid-19th century realist painter who
was later involved in the Paris Commune, refused a Cross of the Legion
of Honour from the Minister of Fine Arts: 'At no time, in no case should
I have accepted it. Still less should I accept it today, when treason multi-
plies itself on all sides and human conscience cannot but be troubled by
so much self seeking and disloyalty... My conscience as an artist
is...repelled by accepting a reward which the hand of government is

pressing upon me—the state is not competent in artistic matters'.[11]

At the same time as the state run academy was losing its credibility and the practice of commission was on its way out, a growing market for fine art was emerging amongst the growing middle classes. Walter Benjamin claims that the French poet Baudelaire was the first to notice these changes:

> The bourgeoisie was in the process of withdrawing its commission from the artist. What steady social commission could take its place? No class was likely to supply it; the likeliest place from which a living could be earned was the investment market... But the nature of the market, where this demand was to be discovered, was such that it imposed a manner of production, as well as a way of life, very different from those of earlier poets.[12]

John Molyneux quite rightly accepts in his article that no one can escape the effects of alienation in their everyday life, but I want to go further and argue with Benjamin that capitalist relations increasingly shaped artistic production itself. Ideally, artists control their output, they create objects in accordance with the laws of beauty, humanising the natural world by transforming matter in a way that expresses their own human essence. The activity of the artist attempts a self expression that is denied in alienated labour. But once artists are at the mercy of the market alienation is reintroduced. The market separates producer from consumer. Ours is a social species that emerged precisely through co-operative labour. The fact that an artist must present a finished product to an audience who passively and privately consume it disrupts the free flow of ideas that are essential to real creativity. Success is judged in terms of sales and prices. In this situation there is massive pressure on the isolated artist to second guess the market, especially if their subsistence depends on sales. Once their work is produced even partially in response to external neccessities, the artist is no longer in control of their own creativity. Many artists must recognise this dilemma. Some admit that potential buyers are very much the focus of their attention. Britart hopefuls Tim Noble and Sue Webster describe in an interview how they bombarded art speculator Charles Saatchi's office with faxes and oddball art objects for months before they finally lured him to their studios where they watched his (favourable) reaction to their work through spy holes they bored in the walls.[13]

In an important sense the capitalist market also denies artists an audience. By robbing the mass of the population of control over their own labour, and therefore over production generally, the market robs us—the potential audience—of much of our artistic or aesthetic capacities. At the same time the market, by atomising consumption and reducing value to a quantitive measure, reduces consumption to mere 'having'; 'Private property has made us so stupid and one sided that an object is only ours when we have it—when it exists for us as capital, or when it is directly possessed, eaten, drunk, worn, inhabited, etc—in short *when it is utilised by us'.*[14] It hardly needs pointing out that questions of ownership and quantitative value dominate in most mainstream consideration of art. Paintings most often make the news because they have broken price records at an auction, or because they have been bought by particular famous (and millionaire) collectors. Meanwhile thousands of key artworks are kept in private homes, government buildings or in cold storage, sometimes to try to lever up values of particular artists. Those of the rest of us who have the time and money are left to catch what glimpses we can of our favourite artists in packed galleries on the weekend or make do with reproductions which drastically diminish any art's impact by removing it from a meaningful context.

All of this has inevitably had a massive impact on artists themselves. The French artist Cézanne, often regarded as a founder of Modernism, fled Paris in the 1860s and became a virtual recluse, railing against the values of the capitalist world of his father who was 'unable to understand anybody except people who worked in order to get rich'.[15] The Impressionists had ambivalent attitudes to the new situation. On the one hand they spent much of their time recording the leisure pursuits of their new clientele, the urban middle classes. Their technique of painting often small canvasses that quickly captured similar scenes in different light was ideally suited to an expanding middle class market. On the other hand the movement started out with a rejection of the stilted and irrelevant classicism of the academy. Its obsession with fleeting appearance was partly a response to new technology, partly a response to rapid social change, but also an expression of isolation:

Impressionism, dissolving the world in light, breaking it up into colours, recording it as a sequence of sensory perceptions, became more and more the expression of a very complex, very short term subject-object relationship. The individual, reduced to loneliness, concentrating upon himself, experiences the world as a series of nerve stimuli, impressions, and moods, as a shimmering chaos, as 'my' experience, 'my' sensation.[16]

Later the more radical fracturing of the plane of illusion initiated by the Cubists suggests a deepening crisis in the artists' relationship with their subject and uncertainty about their role in society. There were many other responses to the same crisis. Some artists defiantly raised the banner of 'art for art's sake' in an attempt to distance themselves from the establishment and from the art market. The Surrealists tried to find refuge from commodification in the pure subjectivity of the subconscious; the Russian Constructivists looked outwards, trying to bind the future of art to mass production. One Marxist critic suggests that 'modern art, in its most heroic moments, is the attempt to escape the reification of existence'.[17] Of course the Modernists were responding to a tremendously turbulent, changing world but their attempts to escape or challenge reification were so radical precisely because art itself was under threat, because artists felt strangled by commodification. Once the bourgeoisie had championed art as a virtuous activity, a token of its commitment to freedom of expression and individuality within a harmonious society, now their own system was threatening to undermine art's very basis.

Throughout the 20th century the struggle for artistic control and authentic expression has continued. From Diego Rivera and Orson Welles to the Sex Pistols, the most challenging artistic products are often the results of a struggle with the hostililty of the culture industry, and all too often, as well, a destructive struggle of the artist with themselves. As a result the commodification of art and the resulting alienation of the artist is a theme running from *All About Eve* to Andy Warhol or Jeff Koons. The story of the artist 'selling out' to the system has become a commonplace. However well they handle it, artists cannot escape their contradictory situation; however much they struggle to conquer a scrap of production for humanity, their product will itself be commodified.

Why does all this matter? First, I think we are deluding ourselves if we believe that any aspect of our lives completely escapes the alienation imposed by capitalist relations. Despite our best efforts, everything from our health to our personal relations is deeply affected by our lack of control over the central social processes. Certainly it is key to socialist politics that under capitalism no part of the production process can escape the alienation imposed by the capitalist market. The priorities of a co-operative or a state run industry or a whole national economy run by the state will ultimately be distorted by the needs of competitive accumulation, and in the process genuine popular control will be lost. It is not the formal ownership of the means of production that matters, but the real relations of production. John's example is a case in point. The man building his garden wall may own the bricks and the garden, but his labour is not unalienated or freely chosen, it is imposed by a system based on the absurdity of privatised domestic life.

Secondly, the idea that artistic production is unalienated could easily encourage an uncritical attitude to art. It could even lead us to accept the simplistic and elitist distinctions between 'high' and 'low' culture so beloved of the right. As well as encouraging critical artists and cultural work we need to be aware that under capitalism a great deal of cultural production in the galleries as well as on TV is quite simply pap, pandering to the most backward ideas generated by the ruling class, reflecting rather than challenging the artist's own alienation.

Finally, it is important to treat art historically. As I have tried to suggest, John's definition of art as unalienated labour tends to take art out of historical development. John points out that Marx warned against crude reductionism when tracing the link between social and economic developments and cultural production. But this warning has to be seen in the context of Marx's repeated insistence that society must be seen as an interrelated totality. This is the very core of his historical method. It would be wrong to argue that art is in long term decline, but John's statement near his conclusion is also unsatisfactory: 'The record of human creativity being what it is, we can reasonably expect to encounter late 20th and early 21st century masterpieces just as there are masterpieces from every century and half century since Giotto and the beginning of the Renaissance'.[18] If only by omission John implies here a trajectory for artistic development separate from the rest of society. Of course, we should avoid oversimplification; human creativity is highly unpredictable, but all art is a product of real people living in concrete circumstances, and wider social developments must impact on it. To see the great period of Modernism in the first 30 years of this century or the late 1960s as cultural high points is not to say art is in terminal decline, just that it thrives on discontent.

1   L Trotsky, *On Literature and Art* (New York, 1977), p106.
2   J Molyneux, 'The Legitimacy of Modern Art', in *International Socialism* 80 (1998), p71.
3   Ibid, p97.
4   K Marx, *Early Writings* (Penguin, 1975), p326.
5   Ibid, p324.
6   Ibid, p326.
7   K Marx, *The Communist Manifesto* (Phoenix, 1996), p8.
8   A Sanchez Vazquez, *Art and Society* (Monthly Review Press, 1973), p218.
9   J Molyneux, op cit, p83.
10   E Fischer, *The Neccessity of Art: A Marxist Approach* (Penguin, 1963), p51.
11   Quoted ibid, p72.
12   Quoted ibid, p69.
13   *The Guardian*, G2 section, 7 December 1998.
14   K Marx, quoted in I Meszaros, *Marx's Theory of Alienation* (London, 1970), p205.
15   Quoted in G Mack, *Paul Cézanne* (New York, 1989), p160.
16   E Fischer, op cit, p75.
17   A Sanchez Vazquez, op cit, p117.
18   J Molyneux, op cit, p97.

REVOLUTIONARY
JOURNALISM

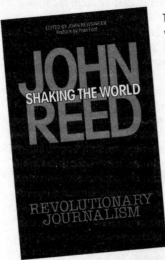

This new volume of John Reeds
writings demonstrates the
breadth of his work: from mass
strikes in the US coal fields to
revolution in the *haciendas* of
Mexico, from the horrors of the
First World War to the storming
of the Winter Palace, John
Reed told the stories of those
fighting back.

Reed analyses the political
strength and weaknesses of
the working class movement,
and his writings are a
testament to the potential of
workers to change the world.

EDITED BY JOHN NEWSINGER
Preface by Paul Foot

BOOKMARKS

Available from Bookmarks,
1 Bloomsbury Street, WC1B 3QE
Phone 0171 637 1848
add £1.80 for p&p

£ 11.95

Fascists brought to book

A review of Pete Fysh and Jim Wolfreys, **The Politics of Racism in France** *(Macmillan, 1998), £45*

PAUL McGARR

'Mobilisation against the Front provokes internal ructions, as the example of the Strasbourg congress clearly illustrates, when tensions between Le Pen and Mégret over the party's elections strategy emerged in public for the first time... These words are being written at a time of renewed hope about the prospects of blocking the fascist revival'.[1]

These are the conclusions of Peter Fysh and Jim Wolfreys' excellent book, whose central theme is the rise of and fight against Europe's biggest Nazi party, France's National Front.

The book was published at the end 1998. It was barely off the presses before the authors' judgement on the possible effects of protests against the Front was confirmed in spectacular fashion. In the last weeks of 1998 the party was ripped apart by internal warfare, and split into two rival groups, one headed by the party's leader, Jean-Marie Le Pen, the other by his deputy, Bruno Mégret.

This infighting often took on bizarre forms. Le Pen denounced Mégret as an 'extremist, racist', while Mégret labelled Le Pen a 'guardian of Nazi ideas'.[2] Physical clashes between supporters of the rival Nazi leaders erupted. In Marseilles, a Mégret stronghold, Le Pen supporters ransacked the local party headquarters.[3] It certainly wasn't a happy Christmas in the Le Pen household. One of his daughters is married to a key Mégret ally and supported the revolt against her father, who publicly railed against this 'family treason'.[4] Le Pen's other daughter backed her father and played a key role in organising the physical eviction of Mégret supporters from the party's national headquarters.[5] The clashes culminated in Le Pen expelling Mégret and a number of his key backers, who—at the time of writing—were in the process of forming a rival party.[6]

These developments are marvellous news for every anti-Nazi. For over a decade now France's National Front has been the biggest and most important Nazi party in Europe, and one to which Nazis elsewhere have looked for inspiration. The fundamental reasons for the rift lie in the two key characteristics that have marked France in recent years. One is the revival of class struggle on a scale bigger than anywhere else in Europe. Beginning with the revolt of Air France workers in 1993, then through a revolt of youth against plans to impose a lower minimum wage, and culminating in the great public sector workers' strikes at the end of 1995, mass struggle and strikes broke the back of the country's right wing government.[7] In 1997 this movement resulted in the election of a left wing coalition government dominated by the Socialist Party, the rough equivalent of Britain's Labour Party. That election has not ended the struggle. Rather, there have been repeated eruptions of struggle—of lorry drivers, the unemployed, a general level of strike action far higher than in other European countries, and, in late 1998, the 500,000 strong revolt by high school students.[8] All this has led to a marked and general shift to the left in France which has posed enormous problems for the National Front, an organisation with little to say when confronted with such struggles.

The second key factor is the upsurge, on a far bigger scale than ever before, of anti-racist and anti-Nazi mobilisations from late 1996 onwards. In the summer of 1996 the Tory government's barbaric treatment of the *sans papiers* (immigrants who had been made 'illegal' by a series of Tory laws) produced a wave of anti-racist mobilisations.[9] Le Pen then sparked new outrage by explicitly saying that he believed in the 'inequality of races'.[10] The anti-racist and anti-Nazi mobilisations began to grow in the wake of these events.[11] By the end of the year virtually every public appearance by a National Front leader was met by impressive mobilisations, such as the one involving 20,000 people protesting against Le Pen in Grenoble in December 1996.

Initially this did not check the growth of the Front. A key turning point came, however, in February 1997, when the National Front won control of the town council in Vitrolles, an overspill town of around 40,000 people just outside Marseilles. This event had an electrifying effect on the atmosphere in the country. For the first time ever the Front won against a single opposition candidate, whereas previously whenever all the established parties had lined up behind a single candidate the Nazis had always been defeated.

The effect was immediate, galvanising a new burst of anti-racist and anti-Nazi activity. Within days of the Vitrolles result a huge movement against the Tory government's proposed new anti-foreigner laws erupted. A march in Paris against the laws attracted 100,000 people, though the real target was as much the National Front as the government's laws. Soon afterwards, at Easter, for the first time ever a national demonstration was called against the National Front when it held its annual congress in Strasbourg. A magnificent 70,000 people (very impressive, given the size and location of the city) marched through Strasbourg. What marked these protests was above all the optimistic feeling and the surge of participation by young people, going way beyond the traditional groups who joined such protests in the years before.[12]

The mobilisations began to crack the Front open, leading to the first signs of a rift between Le Pen and Mégret. The anti-racist and anti-Nazi mobilisations have continued to develop since the election of the Socialist Party government. For example, in the spring of 1998 some 200,000 people, overwhelmingly young, joined anti-Nazi marches around the country when some Tories, facing defeat in important regional council elections, tried to save their skins by making electoral deals with the Front.[13] Even when the French football team won the 1998 World Cup the effect was to reinforce the already developing anti-racist, anti-Nazi mood. Le Pen had earlier attacked the proportion of black and Arab players in the multi-racial French team. Now that rebounded on him, especially as the team's star player, Zinedine Zidane, was the son of an Algerian immigrant and from the northern suburbs of Marseilles (an area which French racists find particularly objectionable). When one million people surged down the Champs Elysées in Paris calling for 'Zidane for President' it helped marginalise the Front further.[14]

Such large scale protests have been mirrored by the development of lively, young and confident local anti-racist and anti-Nazi movements, grouped in various organisations, the most important of which are SOS Racisme, Le Manifeste Contre le Front National, and Ras l'Front.[15] But many more people are involved in various other local groupings, and even in the towns where the National Front runs the councils the resistance has grown and is lively and confident.[16] The social revolts, strikes and the like on the one hand, and the anti-racist and anti-Nazi mobilisations on the other are linked, but are not the same movement and there are important differences in composition and dynamic.[17] But the combined effect has been to hem in and confront the National Front with bigger problems than it has faced for many years, and finally to provoke the internal rift which marked the end of 1998. That rift provides a marvellous opportunity to step up the pressure and begin not only to check, but to start to roll back the Nazi threat in France, a task which if done would be a major blow to their counterparts everywhere.

Whether that happens remains to be seen. It would certainly be foolish to conclude that the Nazi split on its own is sufficient to achieve that end. The history of fascism in the 1920s and 1930s shows that both Hitler and Mussolini survived important splits in their parties in the years before they took power. The National Front is not the threat that either of these were, but it is strong enough and well enough rooted in France to recover from the rift and make further progress, if it is allowed to. A warning came in the first opinion poll taken in France after the split between Le Pen and Mégret.[18] In November 1998, before the split, the Front was running at 16 percent in polls. After the split it was still getting 14 percent, with 10 percent backing Le Pen and 4 percent Mégret.

Thus, despite the internal ructions, the Front remains a worryingly powerful force in France. It has repeatedly won double figures in percentage terms, often over 14 percent, in elections for many years (amounting to some four or five million votes on occasion). It has over 1,000 town councillors around the country, with significant numbers of councillors on every one of the country's important regional councils. It runs the council in four towns, all in the south: Toulon, one of the country's biggest cities, the smaller towns of Vitrolles and Marignane outside Marseilles, as well as the town of Orange. In short, a lot remains to be done in order to take advantage of the setback the Front suffered at the close of 1998.

In successfully doing that it is crucial both to understand what kind of party the National Front is and how it has built, and to overcome some of the weaknesses which have so far marked the opposition to it. Peter Fysh and Jim Wolfreys' book aims to tackle all of these questions, and for anyone wanting to learn and understand these issues and debates there is no better account.

The authors begin by tackling head on one of the central myths of French society, one shared by most of the left and anti-racist organisations and one which has hampered the fight against racism and the National Front. This is the notion that, in the country which gave the world the Declaration of the Rights of Man in the 1789 French Revolution, the traditions of a republic founded on such principles guarantee immigrants fair and equal treatment. In practice this myth has led to serious weaknesses in the anti-racist movement. These include a tendency to talk of the need to defend 'republican values' shared by all 'citizens' against the threat of the National Front. This leads to a political rhetoric and practice which do not correspond to the reality of what the 'republic' has meted out to immigrants and ethnic minorities.

It also leads to a tendency towards alliances involving the right wing which, so the argument runs, can be relied on to rally to 'republican values' against the Front. This wishful thinking is mirrored by a damaging refusal to take up a clear anti-racist stance on several key issues on the grounds that any expression of ethnic or cultural difference threatened the uniformity of France's supposedly democratic republican traditions and institutions.

A glimpse of what this kind of thinking leads to can be seen in the way that much of the left and the anti-racist movement has routinely united behind Tory candidates, and withdrawn their own candidates, to try and electorally check the National Front. This disastrous strategy had a long and terrible history in the 1930s. And in France today such a strategy ignores that Tories have repeatedly been prepared to make deals with the National Front (most notably in helping the Front achieve its first electoral breakthrough in Dreux in 1983 and most recently in the 1998 regional council elections).

Another glimpse of what this kind of thinking has led to can be seen in the disastrous response of much of the left and the anti-racist movement to the question of the right of Muslim schoolgirls to wear headscarves at school. For any anti-racist in Britain it would be axiomatic that one defends this right. In France, however, much of the left and anti-racist movement has attacked and campaigned against it, on the spurious grounds that it somehow threatens the secular nature of the democratic, French republican education system. This has led to the grotesque spectacle of would be anti-racists lining up with racists. At the time of writing teachers in the town of Flers were striking to prevent a 12 year old schoolgirl being allowed into school wearing a headscarf. This strike saw the sickening spectacle of left wingers and Nazis like Mégret taking the same stance.[20]

Peter Fysh and Jim Wolfreys spend the first part of their book looking at the real history of the French state's treatment of immigrants. They utterly demolish the myth of the equal and welcoming republic. They chart how successive waves of immigrants have been subject to barbaric racism. They describe how in the 1880s and 1890s Belgian miners were 'attacked and forced to flee' from France. They chart the savage anti-Semitism which reached a high point in the notorious Dreyfus Affair of the late 19th century. Poles, Italians and, since the Second World War, Arabs and blacks have all been subject in their turn to savage racism.

The authors then turn to examine in detail how in the 1980s the previously marginal National Front made its first breakthrough. In 1981 'the National Front's motley band of a few hundred fascists, racists and ex-collaborators had failed even to get a presidential campaign off the ground, their leader [Le Pen], a verbose former paratrooper, unable to find 500 councillors or parliamentarians to sign his nomination'.[21]

The 1981 election saw the ending of 23 years of Tory rule and the victory of the Socialists under President François Mitterrand. But the hopes for real change millions had in the wake of that election soon

turned to bitter disillusion, as Mitterrand bowed to the bosses and the
bankers. His government pushed through savage cuts, and presided over
soaring unemployment. The Socialists, and shamefully on occasion the
powerful Communist Party too,[22] sought to head off discontent by the
well worn tactic of scapegoating and so whipping up racism.

In 1983 in Dreux, west of Paris, the Tories invited the National Front
to join its electoral list to defeat the Socialists.[23] The authors then chart in
detail the way the Front was able to build on this breakthrough throughout
the following years. It was helped by the appaling reaction of all mainstream politicians, President Mitterrand even deliberately changing the
electoral system in the mid-1980s, hoping to help his party to hang on to
power by 'dividing' the right and allowing the Front to enter parliament.
The authors go through a detailed and informative discussion of the
nature of the National Front vote, demolishing several myths as they go.[24]

They then turn to look at how Le Pen and his party emerged from a
long standing racist and fascist tradition in France. This section has fascinating and informative description and analysis of movements from the
Dreyfus Affair to the 1930s rise of fascism in France, as well as the
important phenomenon of the Vichy regime which collaborated with the
Nazis in the Second World War. From this the authors move on to
describe in detail the origins and emergence of the National Front from
the fragmented Nazi groups in France in the 1970s.

The following chapters, among the best, examine in detail the ideology, strategy and organisation of the Front, and argue polemically and
convincingly that the party is not simply a 'right wing' formation but a
fascist, Nazi party. The authors also chart the various thinkers who have
played a key role in forming the Front's ideas and so they provide a
useful warning to those who think Nazis are simply about skinhead
thugs. To be sure, such thugs are important, but mass parties can only be
built on the basis of some, at least semi-coherent, ideology which,
however filthy, can motivate and attract supporters. The authors also
chart how the Front has had to weld together various strands, which
often sit uneasily with each other inside the party—and which at points
have been and can again be a source of internal tension and splits when
the party is put under pressure.

An important part of the argument focuses on how the Front is not
simply about racism, but provides, or attempts to, a global analysis of
society and offers solutions—from unemployment to housing, from the
world situation to the environment. The way the Front draws in part on a
bastardised version of the 'Marxist' ideology which the French Communist Party espoused, when in the post-war years it was by far the
largest political formation in France, is particularly interesting. The
Front's leaders understood that to build they had to fight on every issue,

and try and achieve hegemony for their ideas. This certainly has been one of their major successes, one boasted about by Bruno Mégret,[25] with mainstream politicians of all hues, including the Socialists, adopting much of the Front's 'discourse'.

'By the early 1990s, references to 'levels of tolerance', the 'invasion' of immigrants, and the 'noise and smell' of foreigners, were no longer the vocabulary of an isolated racist minority. They had become the language of statesmen'.[26] Indeed the three expressions mentioned were used respectively by François Mitterrand, former Tory president Valéry Giscard D'Estaing, and current Tory president Jacques Chirac. This evolution to respectability of many of the Front's ideas and language has been one of the most depressing features of French politics of the last decade and a half.

The authors also explain well how the Front has a conscious technique for cementing its softer periphery to its core ideas:

> *The Front's discourse also deliberately creates a tension between the organisation and its periphery, between 'hard' and 'soft' support, seeking to address sympathisers where they are and take them where the Front wants to go, converting them to the Front's world view and enlarging its core. To this end the party leaders are adept at using language heavy with codes and euphemisms, which asserts and subverts simultaneously, relentlessly pushing debate into previously 'unacceptable' areas. The undisputed master of this technique is Le Pen himself.[27]*

This was exactly the purpose of Le Pen's infamous reference to the Nazi genocide as a 'detail' of history. It 'was no slip of the tongue but a calculated raising of the tension between the NF hard core and the periphery. The remark was bound to provoke condemnations and resignations from the party, but everyone who stayed in had jumped an important hurdle. Some supporters were lost, but others were moulded in the Front's image'.[28]

Although the Front has laid great stress on winning electoral support, the authors argue that ultimately the party sees great social upheaval and possibly violent revolution as the way to power. Le Pen himself argued to the party's youth wing as recently as 1996:

> *Crisis is the great midwife of history. When situations are blocked, it's generally the drive of human nature which forces a breakthrough into new times... Now it is certain that only the National Front can tear this country from decadence... There is a time when all that will end and that will be the revolution. The extreme left is preparing for it... So I believe that you too should prepare yourselves, because at a certain point the worm-eaten structures of our system are going to collapse.[29]*

The authors also show how the Front uses 'front' organisations to systematically implant the party in various sections of society. All this is extremely useful and provides indispensable information and analysis for anyone wanting to understood what the National Front is and how it has been built.

In the following sections of the book the authors turn to look at the development of the anti-racist movement. Particularly useful is their account of the development of organisation and protest among young *beurs*, young people of Arab immigrant origin. They also chart how sections of the established left have sought to manipulate such movements, for instance the Socialist Party in the 1980s, through organisations such as SOS Racisme. The book reveals how many of the established left wing and anti-racist organisations failed to seriously build on these movements of young people of immigrant origin and so failed to weld the resistance to racism and the National Front into an effective force in the 1980s and early 1990s.

The book concludes with an examination of the recent developments discussed earlier, both the success of the National Front in winning control of four councils, and the renewed and more hopeful rise of resistance to the Front and racism more generally. Here the authors are rightly particularly critical of the failure of the leaders of most of the left and the main anti-racist organisations either to correctly understand the nature of the Front or to take a clear stance on anti-racist issues such as the wearing of the headscarf by young Muslim women.

On all these questions Peter Fysh and Jim Wolfreys have provided the clearest, most detailed and sharpest analysis yet, and in that sense I can wholeheartedly recommend this book. There are, however, some criticisms which I feel obliged to make, most of which are, it should be said, not primarily the authors' responsibility.

One is simply the price. At £45 the book is way out of the reach of most people. That of course is the publishers' fault, and one can only hope that they see fit to produce a paperback version at a more affordable price. The price reflects the audience the publishers have in mind—essentially an academic one. They obviously see the book as one for university level politics courses. That aim has imposed certain restrictions on the authors too. In general they work hard, and with success, to avoid falling into the kind of style and language of academicism, and of treating the subject in terms of differing 'models' and 'discourses' that can characterise such sterile discussions. There are some, thankfully few, occasions where this does happen though. And at times one feels a tension in the book between the differing audiences the authors have in mind, or have been obliged to keep in mind.

More important is another problem. In part this is one which confronts anyone writing about contemporary French society. This is how to integrate the various aspects of a total picture—from the social struggles, strikes and the like to the rise of and resistance to the National Front. Naturally in this book the authors focus on racism and anti-racism, the National Front and its opponents. The authors do constantly link their subject to the wider developments in France, but in a way which is sometimes less than satisfactory. So for instance the great public sector workers' strikes of 1995 are there, but only for two paragraphs. Of course the rise of and resistance to racism and the National Front cannot be reduced to a reflex of the wider class struggle. Nevertheless the underlying class struggle is the key factor in understanding the totality of French society and politics. It is the feature which colours and shapes, even if it does not explain, all others.

One example is the impact of the 1995 public sector workers' strikes for the fight against racism. While Le Pen denounced the union leaders at the head of the strikes, and at one point even called for their jailing, an opinion poll showed that a majority of those who had voted for the Front earlier that year supported the strikes. The lesson for how the Front's base could be ripped apart and the party crushed are clear.[30]

Another example is the simple fact that in the waves of struggle and protest of recent years people of whatever colour and ethnic origin have been repeatedly fighting together to defend their common interests. This ranges from white rail workers marching proudly behind a woman of Arab origin at the head of one of the biggest protests in 1995, to the profoundly multi-racial character of the school students' protests in 1998.[31] This struggle on its own does not determine whether the National Front grows or declines, still less how the fight against it and racism more generally develops. But it is a reality that has huge implications for that fight and which shapes the entire society within which that fight takes place.

I feel that the excellent account given in the book would be only strengthened by spending a little more time on linking and relating the issue of racism and the wider struggle. Of course the remit imposed by the publishers no doubt placed sharp limits on how much this would have been possible. One can only hope that the authors, who clearly have the understanding and knowledge to do so, get a chance to round out their analysis in future writings. These few criticisms certainly should not deter anyone from reading what is without doubt the best and clearest account of the politics of racism, the rise of the National Front and the development and weaknesses of the resistance to it I have yet read.

Notes

1   P Fysh and J Wolfreys, *The Politics of Racism in France* (Macmillan, 1998), pp216-217.
2   Agence France Presse news agency report, 'Le Pen Invite Mégret a Créer sa Propre Liste' (Paris, 10 December 1998).

3   Associated Press news agency report, 'Coup de Force pro-Le Pen dans une
      Permanence de Bruno Mégret a Marseille' (Marseille, 11 December 1998).
4   *Libération*, 10 December 1998.
5   Agence France Press news agency report, op cit, 10 December 1998.
6   *Le Monde*, 10-11 January 1999.
7   See C Harman, *International Socialism* 70 (Spring 1996).
8   See for instance *Socialist Worker*, 24 October 1998.
9   Throughout I use the label Tory to characterise the mainstream French right,
      whose most important components are the RPR Gaullist party and the smaller
      UDF coalition. There are important differences between these formations, and
      between both and the British Conservative Party, but the general label 'Tory' is
      accurate enough.
10   *Le Monde*, 21 September 1996 .
11   See P Fysh and J Wolfreys, op cit, p201 onwards.
12   Ibid, and on Strasbourg see *Socialist Worker*, 5 April 1997.
13   See *Socialist Worker*, 28 March 1998.
14   See *Socialist Worker*, 25 July 1998.
15   The first two are linked to various factions within the Socialist Party, the last
      (whose name is a play on the French idiomatic expression *ras l'bol*, meaning to be
      fed up with something) was originated by the far left LCR group although it has
      become broader. There are important differences between these groups, though in
      many areas which group the best people join depends mainly on which is most
      visible and active in that area. Fysh and Wolfreys give a detailed critique of SOS
      and Le Manifeste, see especially chapters 6, 7 and 8, pp143-213.
16   For an account of the resistance to the National Front in Vitrolles see *Socialist
      Worker*, 16 May 1998.
17   But these differences do not mean there are not connections and links. For example,
      at one lycée in the south of Paris the autumn 1998 revolt was initiated and led by
      about five students, who managed to draw in hundreds of their schoolmates. It was
      interesting that this small group had been the only ones at the school who had joined
      the anti-Nazi marches in the spring of 1998, their first ever demonstration.
18   *Libération*, 28 December 1998.
19   A persistent myth in the British media and sections of that in France is that Mégret is
      less a Nazi than Le Pen. This is simply false. His own record and that of the council
      in Vitrolles which he effectively runs show this (see *Socialist Worker*, 16 May 1998).
      The difference between the two Nazis is mainly one of strategy, centring on whether
      or not to seek alliances with Tories as a step towards wielding real power (Mégret's
      line), or whether it is better to stand aloof from that and so better exploit disillusion
      with all established political parties (Le Pen's line). One interesting feature of polls is
      that, among those who say they will vote for the National Front, Mégret has much
      more support than Le Pen among the party's wealthiest supporters, but among the
      poorer that situation is sharply reversed (see *Libération*, 28 December 1998).
20   *Le Monde*, 10-11 January 1999.
21   P Fysh and J Wolfreys, op cit, p1.
22   Ibid, p44.
23   Ibid, p46.
24   Ibid, p68 onwards.
25   Ibid, p130.
26   Ibid.
27   Ibid, p131.
28   Ibid.
29   Ibid, p134.
30   *Socialist Worker*, 16 December 1995.
31   These points are based on personal observation of these protests and movements.

Revisionism revised

A review of Norah Carlin, **The Causes of the English Civil War** (Basil
Blackwell, 1999), £9.99

BRIAN MANNING

Norah Carlin's new book is designed as an introduction for students. It
includes a useful chronological table of events, a glossary of technical
terms, and a guide to further reading. It is distinguished from the usual
run of such books by its attention to theory in its opening and concluding
chapters—the general problem of causation in history, and of the role of
individuals, of ideas, and of social conflicts. In successive chapters on
politics, religion, and economic and social change, she explains clearly
and fairly the 'Whig', 'revisionist', and 'post-revisionist' interpretations
of the causes of the English Civil War. For those who have been fed on a
diet of revisionism, the book provides an informative and insightful cor-
rective. Norah Carlin steers between the excesses of Whiggism and
revisionism and incorporates their researches into a broad and balanced
post-revisionist perspective.

Her philosophical approach is perhaps well illustrated by the following passage:

> It is as difficult to talk of disproving suggested causes of historical events as
> it is to talk of proving them. Existing arguments for a theory can be criticised,
> but it is always possible that better arguments could be put forward, or the
> theory itself developed and improved. That the testing of a theory may lead to
> its being modified rather than abandoned is evident from the whole history of
> natural and social science. That is why it is wrong, for example, to claim that
> the theory of history as class struggle has been 'disproved', though to say that

*this or any other explanation of the civil war is unproven would merely be
stating the obvious.*

On this note class and class struggle disappear from the book.

The book is structured on a similar model to Lawrence Stone's *The
Causes of the English Revolution* (1972), which begins with theory and
then proceeds to arrange causes in three categories—'preconditions', 'precipitants', and 'triggers'. Norah Carlin proceeds from a chapter on 'The
Crisis of 1637-42', which approximates to Stone's 'triggers' (it contains a
helpful critique of the fashionable 'three kingdoms' interpretation—the
interrelationships between events in Scotland, Ireland and England). Next
there are two chapters on the political and religious tensions since 1603,
which are similar to Stone's 'precipitants' (including useful discussions of
whether there were conflicts between 'absolute monarchy' and 'limited
monarchy', and whether the Puritans were 'revolutionaries' or 'conservatives'). And then a chapter on long term economic and social changes,
which may be likened to Stone's 'preconditions' (it involves a discussion of
'backwardness' and 'modernisation'). Of course, the contents and conclusions of Norah Carlin's chapters are very different from Stone's because she
is dealing with historical literature written since his account was published.

The revisionists revealed broad similarities of views on the fundamentals of politics and religion across the ruling class but this is not very
surprising, because that is what one might expect in a ruling class.
Nevertheless, there were divisions in the ruling class, and revisionist
explanations in terms of struggles for place, profit and power, intertwined with differences over policies to be pursued in particular and
immediate situations—practical and tactical rather than ideological—
seem plausible because ruling classes are like that. The basic inadequacy
of revisionism is that its preoccupation with the ruling class makes it difficult to explain why there was a civil war.

Two features in Norah Carlin's account stand out: one is her attention
to the 'middle ground' and the other is her rejection of 'baronial revolt'.
The somewhat baffling and often neglected period between the flight of
the king from London in the face of hostile popular demonstrations in
January 1642, and the first battle of the civil war in October 1642, gains
sense from being seen in terms of a 'battle for public opinion' between
the king and the two houses of parliament. Each side sought to mobilise
the support of 'moderates' and to gain 'as much of the middle ground as
possible'. The 'tone of moderation and the language of consensus' in the
petitions from counties and towns during 1642 helps to explain the adoption by both royalist and parliamentarian leaders of more moderate and
cautious stances. But the pressure to appeal to the moderate middle
ground did not prevent the outbreak of civil war, which began with riots
in the streets before there were any battles between armies, and the

emphasis on the 'middle ground' may savour too much of commentaries on present day English politics.

At the heart of Norah Carlin's interpretation is the view that the civil war is inexplicable as merely a conflict between aristocratic factions. As she explains, 'Petitions and other forms of popular participation in the crisis of 1640-42 must be taken into account in any explanation of the civil war, which was the first conflict of its kind to involve more than a tiny minority of the population in national issues: this is what made it different from the baronial wars of the late middle ages.' She notes that when an arch-revisionist, the earl-historian Conrad Russell, announced in 1973 in *The Origins of the English Civil War* that 'social change explanation of the English civil war must be regarded as having broken down', he added that if a new social change explanation did appear, it would be likely to be based, not on the gentry, but on the 'middling sort'—larger farmers and more substantial craftsmen.

Revisionists adopted the first part of the statement but many, including Russell himself, ignored the second part. However, by getting away from the fruitless disputes about rising and declining gentry, Russell had put his finger on the new social development which made the English Civil War different from medieval baronial conflicts.

Norah Carlin focuses on the 'village and small town elites' consisting of big farmers, traders and substantial craftsmen, who dominated local communities as jurymen, constables, churchwardens and overseers of the poor. This 'middling sort', as they were called at the time, 'had become accustomed to regarding themselves as participants in government rather than the dependants of feudal overlords.' In her conclusion she says that 'it is no accident—though I have to say it was not fully planned in advance—that each of the preceding chapters of the book tends towards one thesis more than any other, that of the importance of the middling sort as a catalyst which polarised the divisions over religion, politics and government in 1641-42'. The independent role of the middling sort provides the basis for the new social change explanation, but Norah Carlin recognises that the middling sort were themselves divided, that they were not all parliamentarians, that many were royalists or neutrals. And there remain questions about the origins of the class hostility between sections of the middling sort and the aristocracy, and about the causes of the divisions amongst the middling sort when it comes to the parties in the civil war, but that is beyond the scope of this book.

Norah Carlin ends her book as follows:

If explanations of the English Civil War in terms of social change are worth pursuing—even for revisionists—it is not because they can reduce the complex question of causality to a simple, agreed formula of bourgeois revolution...

but because they can still attempt to bring together the different strands of explanation; to mediate, in effect, between long-term changes in the economy and short-term political events, and even to aim at that 'integrating or total-ising role' towards which social history has frequently aspired, and repair the breach between the history of society and the history of the state.

This is an important statement and should set the agenda for historians of the English Revolution. I would add, however, that it was the Marxist theory of bourgeois revolution that placed the development of the modern economy, society and state at the centre of historical investigation. Revisionism rejects a key role for the English Revolution in the emergence of modern society, but that is a continuation of a debate, and the question remains, although the answer keeps changing: what did the English Revolution contribute to the development of capitalism? Norah Carlin may be right to reject the answers previously suggested by Marxists, but her book clears the ground of much of the triviality and parochialism of revisionism for renewed efforts to find answers to questions about the role of the English Revolution in the development of the modern economy, society and state—questions central not only to the study of English history but also to the study of world history.

In perspective: Tom Nairn

NEIL DAVIDSON

The 1960s saw an upsurge of separatist nationalisms at the core of the capitalist system, with the movements in Catalonia, Eskudai, Occitania, Quebec, Scotland, Wallonia and Wales all making their first serious impact during that decade. Nationalist demands went on to play a role—although by no means the most important role—in the social upheavals which shook the capitalist system between 1968 and 1976. And although none of them succeeded in establishing new states, several—Catalonia, Quebec and, more recently, Scotland—gained a significant degree of formal autonomy within the state framework of the dominant nation.

These events inspired a number of important studies of nationalism, the majority of which appeared in two clusters. The first appeared between 1977 and 1982 and the second between 1989 and 1992, following a further and, in terms of establishing new states, more successful revival of nationalist aspiration in Eastern Europe. Whatever criticisms might be levelled at these works the best have nevertheless helped to advance our understanding of the phenomenon in important, if partial, ways.[1]

Only a minority of these studies approached the question from an avowedly Marxist perspective. One of them was by the Scottish writer Tom Nairn, who is regarded by many as the foremost modern theoretician of the subject. It is ironic, therefore, that his contribution emphasised the supposed inadequacy of the Marxist tradition as a tool for understanding nationalism, persuading many on the left that, in the famous opening sentence of one key essay, 'The theory of nationalism is Marxism's greatest historical failure'.[2] Most of the essays in which he put forward these arguments were collected in a book first published in 1977 called *The Break-Up of Britain*, but Nairn has recently returned to the subject in a further collection of essays called *Faces Of Nationalism*. On the evidence of this work he no longer considers himself to be any sort of Marxist. Indeed, it is questionable whether he can in any sense still be described as belonging to the left. Nairn is no longer merely a theorist of nationalism—Marxist or otherwise—but a nationalist theorist, advocating nationalism not only for his own nation, but as a universal political programme for the peoples of any potential nation states, in much the same way as revolutionary socialists argue for working class power. The extent to which Nairn has abandoned not only Marxism, but socialism itself, has been missed by both his critics and his supporters.[3] Such misunderstandings should not be allowed to continue. What Nairn advances is nothing less than a theoretical justification for the endless subdivision of the world into competing capitalist nation states.

With the collapse of Stalinism and reduction of social democracy to the most servile position it has ever held in relation to capital, there is a powerful tendency for nationalism to become the vehicle for local opposition to the effects of the global crisis. This is certainly true in Scotland itself, where disillusion with the Blair government has already led to increased levels of support for the Scottish National Party. And while it has never been true that working class support for the SNP necessarily reflected an increased level of nationalism, the danger is that it might become true.[4] Avoidance of that possibility will depend, at least to some extent, on socialists successfully demonstrating to other workers that nationalism is not a solution to our problems but a manifestation of them. One aspect of that demonstration, although by no means the most important one, is to challenge the type of theory advanced by Nairn, where nationalism is presented not only as desirable, but natural and inevitable. The first part of this article therefore traces the development of Nairn's theory of nationalism; the second is a critique of his current position.

Part 1: Nairn's theory of nationalism—from history to human nature

Nairn writes, 'I have never hidden the fact that my own dilemmas and oddities emanate from those of my country, Scotland'.[5] In fact for the first part of his writing career, between 1962 and 1968, Nairn showed no discernible interest in Scotland whatsoever, but devoted his attentions to constructing a thesis on English development with Perry Anderson, then editor of *New Left Review*. This Anderson-Nairn thesis owed far more to

Nairn than to Anderson, at least in its original formulation.[6] For the pur-
poses of this article the most important aspect of the thesis, in relation to
the direction subsequently taken by Nairn, concerns the supposedly
archaic nature of the British state. It was only in this context that Scottish
nationalism, and through it nationalism in general, became the focus of
Nairn's work.

The British state, the working class and the Labour Party

Nairn acknowledges that the combined effects of the Civil War and the
Glorious Revolution were to establish a fundamentally capitalist
economy in England. He argues, however, that because these events
occurred at such an early stage in capitalist development, the English
bourgeoisie, unlike the French Jacobins a hundred years later, did not
require a theoretical understanding of the revolution it had made.
Consequently, the culture of the new ruling class was shaped by the more
established and durable values of the landowning aristocracy who exer-
cised hegemony over their immature junior partner, the bourgeoisie
proper. Unlike other bourgeoisies which followed it to power, the
English bourgeoisie did not become conservative after its economic
power was assured, because it had always been conservative. This state,
consolidated in England by 1688, and, by extension, in Scotland after the
Union of 1707, was therefore pre-modern in structure: 'Although not, of
course, an absolutist state, the Anglo-British state remains a product of
the general transition from absolutism to modern constitutionalism: it led
the way out of the former but never genuinely arrived at the latter'.[7] The
pre-modern character of the British state was preserved beyond the term
of its natural life by the spoils of empire, which rendered any subsequent
'modernisation' unnecessary for the ruling class. Ultimately, however,
when the British state was overtaken by modernising rivals and undermined by the retreat from empire, it entered an almost permanent
condition of crisis which no government of either left or right has been
able to resolve.

   Superficially, this analysis bears some resemblance to that advanced by
Trotsky in his writings on Britain.[8] But although Trotsky was perfectly
aware of what Alex Callinicos calls the 'disadvantages of priority', he also
situated this in the context of the world system and argued that the resul-
tant crisis could be resolved by the working class.[9] Nairn, however, focuses
almost exclusively on the national arena and does not accept the revolutionary potential of the English working class. Here too he regards the
early formation of English capitalism as decisive. The English working
class was formed in the classic period of bourgeois revolution (1789-
1848), but because the English bourgeoisie had already achieved its

victory, the former fought alone for political rights and social progress, unaided by the petty bourgeois insurgencies characteristic of the rest of Europe. Defeated, the working class was forced into a form of 'apartheid': the separateness of a class all too aware of what distinguished it culturally from other classes, but unable to identify the opposed interests which this also involved. Marxism, which might have clarified the situation, was available to the English working class only after it had already entered into its caste-like isolation within bourgeois society.

According to Nairn these characteristics were inherited by the political party which is usually thought to speak for English workers. Dominated by a bureaucratic gradualist right, besotted by the supposed wonders of the British constitution, and opposed only by a succession of moralistic but impotent 'lefts', the Labour Party was a useless instrument for achieving socialism. Yet his critique was not based on the premise that Labour had betrayed its supporters, but rather that it had all too faithfully reflected their lack of class consciousness.

It is not my intention to subject Nairn's analysis to detailed criticism here, since a massive literature exists which does precisely that.[10] The main theme, however, is clear: the British state is an archaic formation in deep crisis, but which nevertheless exercises such a hold over society that no force exists which can destroy or even restructure it.

Tartan waistcoats and the dreams of May

In the beginning Scottish nationalism offered no prospects of playing a modernising role. Throughout the 1960s the Scottish National Party had been gathering electoral support almost unnoticed by political commentators of left or right. In 1961 their candidate polled a respectable 18.7 percent of the vote at a by-election in Glasgow Bridgeton. The following year SNP Chairman William Wolfe came second to Labour candidate Tam Dayell in West Lothian with 23 percent of the vote—more than the Conservatives and Liberals combined. Finally, in November 1967, Winifred Ewing won a by-election in the previously safe Labour seat of Hamilton, beating Labour into second place by 18,397 votes to 16,598.[11] Nairn drew attention to the significance of these developments in an article for *New Left Review* which appeared in 1968, 'The Three Dreams of Scottish Nationalism', which was resolutely hostile to the nationalism of the SNP.

Nairn argues that the Scots have undergone three successive attempts to define their identity. The first of these was Calvinism. Nairn correctly argues that the 'rising bourgeoisie' did not initiate the Reformation of 1559. It was to remain inconsequential for another century and only achieved full dominance after 1746. Instead, the Church of Scotland acted both as a substitute for absent state power and as the unifying factor in a civil society. After the Union with England of 1707, the kirk was, along with the legal system, one of the institutions specifically preserved from the dissolution of the state. Consequently, it became the main vehicle through which a separate national identity was maintained.

The second attempt was not, as might be expected, the Enlightenment, in which Scotland attained greater eminence than any nation apart from France, but Romanticism. The leading figures in the Enlightenment were not concerned with Scottishness, but identified themselves with the British nation politically and were concerned with discovering universal laws of human development: 'While the Enlightenment was only an episode, Romanticism entered her soul'.[12] But the way in which it did so was markedly different from that of other European nations. Whereas, in Italy or Germany, Romanticism was part of the formation of national identity, in Scotland, particularly in the work of Sir Walter Scott, it acted as another substitute for it.

The third attempt was—or more precisely, is—the modern national consciousness of industrial Scotland, which Nairn sees as being positively schizophrenic. One element is the debased romanticism of a popular culture which then still revolved around tartan and bagpipes, whisky and haggis, the Loch Ness Monster and Greyfriars Bobby, Calvinism and a militarist celebration of the Scottish contribution to the British Empire. The other is the 'ethereal tartanry' of the intelligentsia, which begins as a rejection of such images of Scotland, but ultimately reproduces them at a more refined level.

Nairn notes that the SNP represents 'bourgeois nationalism', a political formation which socialists have seen as historically justified in only two situations—first, during the original bourgeois revolutions which completed the transition from feudalism to capitalism, and second as the means by which mainly non-European peoples have mobilised to liberate themselves from the imperialism of these original capitalist nation states. Scotland had long since accomplished the first and consequently has no requirement for the second.[13] Nevertheless, Nairn argues that there are two reasons why the national aspirations of the Scots must be supported. First, 'as a blow against the integrity of British imperialism' and secondly, 'because it represents some transfer of power to a smaller arena'.[14] The first is certainly a legitimate reason for not opposing Scottish separatism; the second is more problematic, suggesting that a government in Edinburgh might be politically, rather than merely geographically, closer to the people who elected it than one in London. However, instead of supporting the SNP, Nairn argues Scottish socialists must develop their own form of nationalism with which to oppose bourgeois nationalism: 'Is it really impossible that

Scotland, which has dwelt so long and so hopelessly on the idea of a nation, should produce a liberated, and revolutionary nationalism worthy of the name and the times?'[15]

The events of May 1968 in France had an effect on Nairn. He wrote a collaborative contribution to the literature of May during a struggle in which he was personally involved: the occupation of Hornsey College of Art in London. In a revised version of 'The Three Dreams of Scottish Nationalism', included in the 1970 collection *Memoirs Of A Modern Scotland*, in which the counterposition of revolutionary socialism to Scottish nationalism is strengthened still further, Nairn notes that the 'tartan waistcoated bourgeoisie' had not remained unchallenged: 'I do not want to turn aside either from Scotland's native tradition of working class protest, John Maclean, Clydeside radicalism, or the communist tradition of the miners.' The problem was that these alternatives had never come close to dislodging their class enemies. Bourgeois nationalism, however, was a false solution to the problem, proposing as it did a false unity of interest between different classes. Nairn goes on to argue that the Scots have two choices, one of which leads into 'the prison of an archaic bourgeois nationality', and the other to a 'revolutionary' consummation which would destroy the prison and lead towards a 'real, meaningful future existence'. Nairn makes it clear that the latter possibility has been inspired by 1968:

> *I for one am enough of a nationalist, and have enough faith in the students and young workers of Glasgow and Edinburgh, to believe that these forces are also present in them. I will not admit that the great dreams of May 1968 are foreign to us, that the great words on the Sorbonne walls would not be at home on the walls of Aberdeen or St Andrews, or that Linwood and Dundee could not be Flins and Nantes. Nor will I admit that, faced with a choice between the Mouvement du 22 mars and Mrs Ewing, we owe it to 'Scotland' to choose the latter.*

This counterposition of a specifically Scottish socialist alternative to the bourgeois nationalism of the SNP constituted Nairn's first concession to the latter. Why did 'the great dreams of May 1968' have to be considered in a purely Scottish context in the first place? Nevertheless, the overall tone of the piece is clearly aligned with the revolutionary movement of the time. This was not to last.

European integration and British disintegration

In 1972, at a time when the class struggle in Britain was at the highest level since 1919, Nairn devoted an article, comprising the whole of *New*

Left Review 75, to a critique of the dominant left positions on British entry to the Common Market, as the European Union was then known. His central argument was that although there had indeed been a major upturn in the industrial class struggle, it had failed to find new organisational forms. At the same time the Labour Party, the TUC, the Communist Party and the revolutionary left were all engaged in channelling the massive levels of worker discontent into the relatively safe question of opposition to British entry to the Common Market, tying the left to supporting British nationalism.[16]

Two aspects of this argument should be noted as foreshadowing his current position. The first is the assertion that when the British left counterpose socialist internationalism to the capitalist Common Market, they are 'really' using this as a cover for defending the integrity of the British imperialist state. The second is that Nairn now sees the only possibility of transforming the British state in any direction as coming from forces external to the state itself—in this case the supra-national institutions of Western European capital.

It was in this context that Nairn returned to the subject of Scottish nationalism, in the aftermath of the second important SNP by-election victory, at Govan during November 1973. The tone was now very different. The article in question, 'Scotland and Europe', which appeared in *New Left Review* early in 1974, is much more concerned with a historical analysis of Scottish distinctiveness than the nature of the SNP and, in this respect, it may be the best thing he has ever written. Nairn begins with the central problem: the absence of Scottish nationalism during the periods when other national movements dominated European politics. Why did it only take political form in the 1920s, at the very moment the modern European state system had taken shape? Only a detour through a general theory of nationalism gave Nairn the answer. He wrote that, 'Nationalism, unlike nationality or ethnic variety, cannot be considered a "natural" phenomenon.' Instead, it must be defined as 'mobilisation against the unpalatable truth of grossly uneven development'.[17] The modern capitalist world emerged from the combined pressures exerted by the British Industrial Revolution and the French Revolution. These forced all other states into copying their achievements in order to compete effectively with or be dominated by their more advanced rivals. But this could not be simply an acceptance of 'progress' as defined by the front runners, it also necessitated a rejection of progress in the terms on which they offered it. This process, which is more or less parallel with that of the bourgeois revolution, spread out from the unifications of Germany and Italy during the 1860s to contemporary national liberation movements in places as different as Ireland and Bangladesh.

Where did Scotland fit in to this dualist view of historical development?

Uniquely, Nairn argued, through the Union of 1707, Scotland 'exploited' the achievements of the English bourgeois revolution, thus entering—indeed, helping to define—the advanced world of capitalism. Scottish capitalist development was fully attained before the age of nationalism began and so, although Scotland had all the ingredients necessary for a nationalist movement—a rising bourgeoisie, an intelligentsia, a popular tradition of hostility to England, a national church—no social class required such a movement.

The political implications of this analysis did not become clear until the following year, when an essay by Nairn called 'Old and New Scottish Nationalism' appeared in a collection called *The Red Paper On Scotland*, edited by the current Chancellor of the Exchequer in an earlier, more left wing incarnation. Nairn now argued that, like several other areas in Western Europe, Scotland was experiencing the rise of what he called neo-nationalism. In the Scottish case, the arrival of American based oil companies in the North Sea had provided a functional equivalent of the imperialist intrusions which had provoked 'modernising', 'developmental' nationalisms of which Scotland had previously no need. Here Nairn dismisses the earlier analysis of 'Three Dreams', which assumed that Scottish self-determination would come as a result of socialism, as based on 'two misjudgments': 'overestimate of socialist potential and underestimate of capitalism's ability to mutate further'. According to Nairn, 'the left had pinned too much faith on the rationality of working class based struggle (understood as a potentially international force), and far too little upon the non-rational strengths of nationalism.' In these circumstances socialists had little option but to accept the continued influence of nationalism: 'In my view it has become totally inadmissible to oppose such tendencies in the name of an abstract internationalism, a universal socialist or class struggle which exists only in aspiration'.[18]

These words were written in 1975, during which the revolutionary period which opened in 1968 was drawing to a close. Nairn seems to have seen Scottish nationalism as a substitute for the inability of the working class to destroy the British state: 'More than any other factor, more even than the miners' strikes of 1972 and 1974, it has exposed the senility of the old consensus and its two party system'.[19] These claims are quite astonishing. The British state has only been in actual crisis (as a result of its internal contradictions, rather than war) on three occasions this century: first between 1910 and 1914, then in 1919 and finally between 1969 and 1974. On each occasion Scottish nationalism trailed some way after the class and anti-imperialist struggles in Ireland in the list of factors causing this crisis.

In practice, Nairn treats the state in classically liberal fashion, as an autonomous body exercising a constricting power over society. His hatred of this state is undeniable, but it springs less from the fact that it exists to run society in the interest of the bourgeoisie, as from its inability to 'modernise'. From this perspective events at the summit of politics which threaten the supposed sovereign power of the British state take on a special significance which workplace struggles do not immediately seem to possess.

In keeping with his instrumental view of nationalism, Nairn does not indulge in the glorification of Scottish history in the manner of more conventional Scottish nationalists. Indeed, if anything, he achieves the almost impossible task of both exaggerating the backwardness of pre-Union Scotland and the mindlessness of tartanry.[20] For this he was denounced by two self proclaimed nationalist 'philosophers', Craig Beveridge and Ronald Turnbull. These authors draw a distinction between those, like Nairn, whom they see as 'fighting for a socialist future' within which nationalism is simply a 'tactical possibility', and those, like themselves, who are fighting for 'a culture, a history, [and] a people as an integral part of a socialist *politique*'.[21] In the mid-1970s this distinction was certainly still relevant. Nairn maintained that Scottish nationalism should be supported because it offered the possibility of a alternative road to socialism to the hopelessly economistic struggle waged by miners and the like. In 1977 he made explicit the perspective implied by privileging Scottish (and to a lesser extent, Welsh) nationalism over the class struggle:

> *The fact is that neo-nationalism has become the gravedigger of the old state in Britain, and as such the principal factor making for a political revolution of some sort—in England as well as the small countries. Yet because this process assumes an unexpected form, many on the metropolitan left solemnly write it down as a betrayal of the revolution.*
>
> *...The reason is that proletarian socialism is supposed to be the gravedigger, and no-one else will do. So they tell the nationalists to drop their shovels and put up with the pathetic limits of 'devolution': the revolution will solve their problems along with the others. Meanwhile they should wait until the time is ripe—ie the time for socialism—taking a firm grip on their petty bourgeois, backward looking impulses. The essential unity of the UK must be maintained till the working classes of all Britain are ready.*[22]

Nairn originally developed a general theory of nationalism in order to explain the particular Scottish variant. Now he moved back from the particular to the general, taking with him the pessimism about working class politics which characterised 'Old and New Scottish Nationalism'. In 'The Modern Janus', also written in 1975, he summarised his views as they had evolved over the previous seven years. First, it is important to note that Nairn does not pretend that all nationalisms—or indeed, any nationalisms—are wholly virtuous. While recognising that judgements have to be made about specific cases based on political criteria, Nairn maintained that this was not decisive. Ultimately, all nationalisms share the same contradictory nature:

> *...nationalism can in this sense be pictured as like the old Roman god, Janus, who stood above gateways with one face looking forward and one backwards. Thus does nationalism stand over the passage to modernity, for human society. As human kind is forced through its strait doorway, it must look desperately back into the past, to gather strength wherever it can be found for the ordeal of 'development'.*

Here is the familiar analysis of the spread of nationalism after 1789 as a necessary response on the part of modernising elites to the uneven development of capitalism. Now it is accompanied with a dismissal of the independent role of the oppressed: 'The new middle class intelligentsia of nationalism had to invite the masses into history; and the invitation had to be written in a language they understood.' Later in the same essay Nairn argues that nationalism is inescapable in the core and periphery of the system alike: 'There was never any chance of the new universal class which figured in the Marxist doctrine emerging as "proletarians" rather than as "Germans", "Cubans", "Irishmen" and so on.' This is because:

> *Nationalism could only have worked, in this sense, because it actually did provide the masses with something real and important—something that class consciousness postulated in a narrowly intellectualist mode could never have furnished, a culture which however deplorable was larger, more accessible, and more relevant to mass realities than the rationalism of our Enlightenment inheritance. If this is so, then it cannot be true that nationalism is just false consciousness. It must have a functionality in modern development, perhaps one more important than that of class consciousness and formation within the individual nation states of this period.*[23]

Nairn attempted to put his theory into practice by joining the Scottish Labour Party, the organisation set up by Labour MPs Jim Sillars and Alex Neil in January 1976. In retrospect, the brief history of the SLP, whose membership never rose above 1,000, shows that there is little room in Scotland for a reformist party straddling the ground between the Labour Party and the SNP. For Nairn, the attempt by that organisation to combine socialism and nationalism in equal measures was its strength, as, 'We have to fight coherently on both fronts'.[24] But events in Scotland led Nairn to abandon the socialist front.

By 1978 the Labour government had been reduced to a minority in the House of Commons and was under extreme pressure both from socialists opposed to its attacks on trade unions and the welfare state, and a resurgent Conservative Party under Thatcher for not attacking trade unions and the welfare state hard enough. The minority Labour government was partly reliant on SNP votes at Westminster, and therefore needed simultaneously to undermine nationalist support while appearing to meet nationalist demands. The trick was to be performed by offering the Scots a largely powerless Assembly which, Labour ministers hoped, would nevertheless meet national aspirations sufficiently for Scottish independence to be seen off, at least for the duration of the immediate crisis. The scheme might have worked, but it was sabotaged from inside the Labour Party itself. The Scotland Bill of July 1978 offered administrative devolution, providing the proposal was backed by a majority of the Scottish voters in a referendum. George Cunningham, a Scottish MP who sat for the London constituency of Islington, introduced an amendment to the Bill which required 40 percent of the Scottish electorate to support it in a referendum, rather than a simple majority of those voting. The subsequent campaign saw the Labour Party split down the middle, with one wing supporting the 'Labour Vote No' committee and the other the 'Labour Movement Yes' campaign.

Outside the Labour Party, the left in Scotland showed far greater unanimity in supporting devolution. The Communist Party of Great Britain had already adopted a policy of 'national self-determination' for Scotland in 1964. Among the orthodox Trotskyist organisations the International Marxist Group and supporters of *Militant* supported devolution. Only the SWP stood aside from this unusual display of left unanimity, standing on what might be called a position of 'malign abstentionism'.[25] However, the point is not that the SWP took a wrong position on the issue—the lesson was subsequently learned—but that, contrary to what Nairn has subsequently claimed, the majority of the left supported devolution.

In the end only 32.9 percent of the electorate voted 'Yes'. Indeed, only 63.8 percent turned out to vote at all. It is possible that the concerns of most Scots, certainly most Scottish workers, were elsewhere. The campaign had been conducted in the aftermath of the last great general wave of industrial struggle in Britain to date, the so-called Winter of Discontent, when the pressure from below against wage restraint finally forced the union leaderships to call action against the Labour government. Unlike the strikes between 1969 and 1975, however, these strikes were not imbued with feelings of optimism and hope but pessimism and despair. The election of a

Tory government was felt by many to be inevitable months before the poll was announced. In the event, the SNP reaction to the inevitable repeal of the Scotland Act was to bring a motion of censure, supported by the Tories, which saw the government defeated, a general election called, and the election of the first Thatcher government.

As Andrew Marr has written, 'Part of the bitterness and disillusion with which the Scottish political and journalistic world greeted the result [of the referendum]...reflected the amazement of Scotland's suburban leftish-leaning establishment that their views were not shared more widely throughout the country'.[26] At the time Nairn reflected these feelings of 'bitterness' and 'disillusion', but did not, however, blame the Scottish people for their lack of enthusiasm for devolution. For Nairn the blame lay elsewhere, with the left.

In a new endnote to an essay called 'Internationalism: a Critique', written after the 1979 referendum, Nairn writes of the fiasco: 'In very adverse circumstances, a small majority had actually voted in favour of the Labour government's devolution Act; and yet had been frustrated by a mixture of old imperialism and the "internationalism" analysed here'.[27] There is something in this. 'Old imperialism' is straightforward enough. Labour right wingers like George Cunningham and Tam Dayell were then, and are now, committed to defending the integrity of the British imperialist state against any form of constitutional reform, no matter how superficial, on the grounds that it will inevitably lead to separatism. What about 'internationalism'? The same case was essentially made by the Labour left, although with different emphases. As Eric Heffer wrote in his memoirs, 'I feared that devolution for Scotland and Wales would weaken Britain as a united economic unit and be detrimental to socialism as a whole'.[28] Nairn's error is to assume that every objection to Scottish nationalism must universally be based on 'Unionist' support for the British state.

Reviewing the arguments of *The Break-Up Of Britain* in October 1981 Nairn wrote of his attempt to steer a course between two 'primitive but vigorous opponents' both advancing equal and opposite errors: 'On one side a bourgeois nationalism denied region and class altogether; on the other a lumpen socialism denied nationality any progressive significance whatever (unless its frontier ran through the middle of the English Channel).' He nevertheless refuses to see that any of the critics who were alarmed at 'the spectacle of a Marxist sympathising with the notoriously bourgeois nationalism of the SNP' might have had a point, dismissing their objections as 'bilge, the product of reheated stereotypes and the sermonising impulse so important to a frustrated left.' For Nairn the 'majority' who did not awaken to national consciousness, which presumably includes most of the working class, were afflicted by 'a peculiarly Scottish torpor' comprised of 'respectable servility' and a 'Jekyllish conformism and a fear of reversion to being "natives".'[29]

Nairn allowed that, just possibly, a combination of the revived Labour left, then mobilised around the Alternative Economic Strategy, and the more left wing nationalism he saw developing in Scotland, might point towards a socialist solution to the crisis of the British state.[30] Such hopes were quickly dashed. The Bennite left had already peaked by the time these cautious hopes were expressed in late 1981 and the left within the SNP, in the shape of the '79 Group, was expelled during the same year. Scottish nationalism, far from recovering from the disaster of 1979, retained a low level of support until the third Conservative electoral victory in 1987 brought a new dimension of support which extended far beyond the ranks of the SNP. Long before then, however, Nairn's fundamental pessimism reasserted itself. A dispute within the editorial board of *New Left Review* in 1982 resulted in a split, caused partly by personality differences, but also by the question of whether the decline of Stalinism, both as state power in the East and working class organisation in the West, could herald the revival of a genuine revolutionary movement. Anderson and the editor, Robin Blackburn, were at this stage still committed—albeit somewhat abstractly—to a perspective which saw such a development as being possible; Nairn sided with the faction which held that it was not, and after they lost the fight, he resigned in solidarity with them.[31]

The remainder of the decade was largely taken up with writing his book on the British monarchy, *The Enchanted Glass* (1988), whose central thesis concerning the ideological dominance of the Windsors has been so comprehensively refuted by events that further comment is unnecessary. It was at this point, however, that Nairn resumed his engagement with nationalism proper. The majority of the essays contained in *Faces Of Nationalism* were written after the Eastern European revolutions of 1989 and they cast their shadow over its contents. Here Nairn raises to new extremes all the positions which he had previously held in earlier writings. Three themes have now emerged full blown which until now had only been hinted at; the identification of Marxism with Stalinism, the introduction of 'human nature' as an explanatory framework for the existence of nationalism and the consequent rejection of internationalism even as a theoretical possibility.

Uncovering secret Stalinists

The extent to which even nominally anti-Stalinist socialists like Nairn tended to identify the Stalinist states with socialism was only fully revealed after their collapse, when he performed the familiar exercise of rejecting Marxism along with the states which described themselves as Marxist.

This then allows him to equate fascism and 'communism': 'Attempts to realise these prophesies—and the struggle between them—have accounted for much of the past century. Fortunately they ran out of steam before annihilating the species. But does even the most fervent optimist think this could not have happened?'

Nairn pursues his attack on Marxism into the work of his one time inspiration, Antonio Gramsci. According to Nairn, Gramsci is not the advocate of civil society for which he is taken. On the contrary, Gramsci is alleged to have seen his purpose as being to destroy civil society:

> *The circumstances of censored notebook composition compelled a detour through...pluralism, and the avoidance of an overtly anti-statist and anti-national rhetoric. But the point of it was to lay the foundations of the standard internationalist state of Third International times: **il moderno principe** or radically Leninist polity within which society would be reconfigured to suit the vision of a commanding elite.*

Nairn does note, in passing, that Gramsci was in fact opposed to the direction which Stalin took the USSR and the Communist International during the 1920s and 1930s, and that this was one of the reasons why socialists in the 1960s were attracted to his work. Nairn now reveals that they were mistaken: 'Behind any disenchantment with "crude" Russian hegemony lay a more powerful will towards, in Harding's words, "a transcendent tactic and sublime goal" in the sky of the new proletarian enlightenment'.[32] Gramsci is therefore said to have harboured a monolithic 'statist' agenda behind the superficially open concepts employed in his prison notebooks—a position which echoes the earliest Cold War assessments of his work by American academics.[33]

Humans need nations

It seems likely that the events of 1989-1991 simply gave Nairn an occasion, rather than a reason, for publicly abandoning Marxism and its associated political commitments. Accordingly, he no longer argues for nationalism as an alternative road to socialism. He now argues that it is the fate of humanity because it corresponds to the requirements of human nature. This is extreme, even by Nairn's previous standards. He rightly dismisses the notion, associated with currently fashionable cant about globalisation, that the nation-state has run its course. However, his alternative is based on the opposite and equally damaging error. Discussing the new wave of nationalisms which have arisen since 1989, he writes, 'If...people have not been able to help being like that (inventors of cultural contrasts, antagonistically differentiated, etc) then what is to prevent blood and accursed "human nature" coming into their own once again?' If true, these remarks would be the occasion for despair. But Nairn is neither despairing nor depressed, for such responses would be the result of misunderstandings. Nationalism, in this account, has been the downfall of empire, from the Dutch revolt against Spanish absolutism in the 16th century to the Eastern European revolt against Russian totalitarianism in the 20th. For this reason, it has to be welcomed, despite its continual splitting up of existing states: 'If the role of primordial human nature was greater than [Gellner's theory of modernisation] allows, however, then may it not be that what saved us [ie from Stalinism—ND] may also be condemning us to an indefinite futurity of differentiation?'[34]

Although he circles evasively around the issue, distancing himself from the 'dreadful simplicities of racism and ethnic nationalism', Nairn ultimately opts precisely for this oldest of reactionary creeds: 'Any new paradigm depends, in other words, on establishing a more plausible link between biology and kinship on the one hand, and the world of politics, nation states and resurgent nationality on the other'.[35] To this end, he expects the Human Genome Project, and other research into the 'life sciences' more generally, eventually to prove the link between biology and nationhood. The same point was made more simply in an article from 1992 not reproduced in this collection:

...if diversity was never merely a 'given', in the meaningless accident sense, a different light must be thrown upon its persistence. If internal species-diversity through cultural means has always been 'human nature', presumably it will go on being so—in a way that has nothing to do with ideology of blood or race.[36]

It should be noted that Nairn does not attempt to excuse what he calls 'blots, excrescences or failures' in the record of nationalism since 1989. He merely considers that 'the bombardment of Dubrovnick or the political rape of Muslim women' are a price worth paying for the downfall of the USSR and the other oppressor states of the Stalinist bloc: 'Insistence that the small battalions are likely to be "on the whole" better than the large—particularly the multi-ethnic large—does not imply there can be no pathology of the ethnic, or no cases where nationalists are wrong'.[37]

In fact, Nairn does attempt to explain the genocidal aspects of nationalism. The problem, he claims, is not nationalism as such, but *ethnic* nationalism, particularly where it used to mobilise a peasant population whose way of life is under threat from 'modernisation'. On this basis, Nairn not only seeks to explain the Cambodian and Rwandan massacres, but the lack of violence in the history of Scottish and Welsh nationalism compared to that of rural Ireland.[38] In a more recent article in *New Left Review* he extends this analysis to include the rise of Nazi Germany, identifying the centrality of rural Bavaria and its capital, Munich, in inculcating Fascism. Indeed, in combination with a range of other factors Nairn treats the persistence of peasant life and its forced entry into modernity as the prime cause of what he calls 'nationalist disasters'. Munich was 'a town of peasant culture', Cambodia and Rwanda were 'virtually 100 percent peasant', Bosnia and Serbia were 'less touched by the process of halting industrialisation than many outside observers realised', and so on.[39]

In reality, these cases have little in common. The genocide in Rwanda took the form of an inter-peasant conflict about access to land, and was neither a rural revolt against the towns nor a national struggle in any recognisable sense. Cambodian Stalinism certainly embodied a ferocious anti-urban bias, but the victims of Khmer nationalism were not, in the main, killed because of their ethnicity, but because of their supposed opposition to the New Order: most of the bones now preserved in Tual Sleng extermination centre are of 'ethnic' Khmers. Indeed, the second greatest example of systematic internal violence in the 20th century (after Nazi Germany), Stalinist Russia between 1929 and 1956, can scarcely be said to have rested on peasant support, since at one level the industrialisation of the Soviet Union can be seen as a civil war waged by the bureaucracy *against* the peasantry. The reason why Irish nationalism has repeatedly been forced to resort to violence is not the consequence of peasant trauma at modernisation (in 1798!) but a response to the institutionalised violence of the British state and its Orange offshoot—and this is a violence which the Scots certainly have been responsible for exercising.

In short, the entire argument is an exercise in apologetics: tragically, these pre-modern peasants are susceptible to ethnic mobilisation which can lead to genocide; happily, we modern urbanites have attained a level of civic nationalism which allows us to engage in democratic state-building without relapses into tribal barbarism. But the distinction between 'civic' and 'ethnic' nationalism is extremely dubious. 'Ethnicity' is as much an invented condition as 'race' (or indeed, 'nation'); political conflicts *create* ethnic divisions, not the other way around, and there is *no* nationalism which could not begin to adopt 'ethnic' distinctions in situations of social crisis. Given the way in which Scotland (and the Scottish national consciousness) has been implicated in the atrocities of the British Empire and the racism which accompanied them, can Nairn be so sure that these elements would not rise to the surface of Scottish Nationalism if economic conditions were bad enough? The legacy of Britishness is not escaped so easily.

This is why the question of German fascism is important to Nairn's argument: Nazi Germany, for Marxists, is an example of a modern, developed capitalist power succumbing to extreme right wing nationalism in its fascist form. If it can be shown to be the product of peasant backwardness, rather than modern capitalist society, however, then nationalism emerges without responsibility for the Second World War and the Holocaust. Now, as Zygmunt Bauman has pointed out, the anti-Semitism which formed the core of Nazi ideology was, as Nairn suggests, a form of resistance to modernity.[40] But this only explains the *origins* of anti-Semitic ideology, not how significant sections of the German nation, including its most 'modern' sections, could succumb to it. As Geoff Eley has written, against earlier attempts to blame Nazism on supposed German backwardness, the answer lies 'in the immediate circumstances in which the Nazis came to power—namely, the successive conjunctures of the First World War, the post-war crisis of the 1917-23, and the world economic crisis after 1929'.[41] Twenty years before the Nazis came to power, Germany as a whole had long since left 'rural backwardness' behind:

In 1913, Germany was producing two-thirds of all European steel...double the British figure and not far short of the American one. She produced almost as much coal as Great Britain, and took many European markets from her.

More importantly, the class structure changed as a result. In 1880 German society was one in which the majority of the population worked on the land and industry was confined to small workshops:

In 1914, not much more than one third worked in agriculture (thirty five percent), almost two fifths in industry. But within industry there was a great change over from small firms employing a handful of workmen to middle sized and, most spectacularly of all, very large concentrated firms whose huge ugly factories dominated the Ruhr, Silesia, Saxony.[42]

In short, Germany was not a society in transition to modernity but one which had arrived. Bauman's comments on the Holocaust are also appropriate to describe the frenzy of German nationalism which accompanied it: 'The Holocaust was born and executed in a modern rational society, at the high stage of our civilisation and at the peak of human cultural achievement, and for that reason it is a problem of that society, civilisation and culture.'[43]

Nairn seems to believe that, against the 'big battalions', small is always beautiful. 'Regrettably', he writes of Italian and German unification in the 19th century, 'both these great and exemplary unification projects ended in fascism'.[44] The corollary of this is his enthusiasm for 'micro-states', a category in which he numbers Andorra, Gibraltar, Hong Kong, Jersey, Liechtenstein, Malta, Monaco and San Marino.[45] Ulster, it is hinted, may also belong in this company. Is this the future of the international state system? There are at least three reasons why this is extremely unlikely.

First, the list itself is extremely heterogeneous. Hong Kong was the creation of British imperialism (as are those other non-European 'micro-states' which Nairn unaccountably omits—Kuwait and the other Gulf dictatorships); Singapore developed out of the retreat from empire; both economies are primarily geared to the export market which developed out of the post-war boom. The European examples are remnants of the tiny pre-capitalist principalities which once covered Europe, and which have established themselves as off-shore tax havens. The circumstances in which these quite different states came into being are unlikely to be repeated.

Secondly, these are not nations. The discussion of 'micro-states' is the one point in the book where Nairn blurs the difference between states and nations—with good reason, for the notion of a Monacoan nationalism is implausible to say the least. But so too, more importantly, is a Hong Kong nationalism. All of the forces which opposed the Chinese takeover, bourgeois and proletarian, did so on class, not nationalist grounds. The national identities which have developed in 'micro-states' tend to be those of the dominant power which guarantees their existence. In Ulster and Gibraltar (and the Falkland Islands) it is British nationalism which holds sway, not that of the territory itself.

Thirdly, there is no reason to suppose that the future direction of nationalism will only involve the disintegration of existing nation states. It is at least as likely that nationalism will find expression in policies of aggressive integration. In this respect the failed Iraqi attempt to absorb Kuwait and the successful Chinese attempt to absorb Hong Kong reveal the shape of things to come as much or more than the splitting of Czechoslovakia into its component parts.

What this section of the book does reveal, however, is another element which Nairn expects to form an eternal aspect of human existence. At one point he draws a revealing comparison between nationalism and the state, both of which are 'very unlikely to wither away'.[46] His acceptance of the continued existence of the state is of course a necessary concomitant to his argument concerning the inescapability of nationalism but Nairn's eternal state is a capitalist state. Nairn lets this slip during a discussion of the components of the Eastern European revolutions:

There was a popular, democratic rebellion against one party autocracy and state terror. There was an economic revulsion against the anti-capitalist command economies which for forty years had imposed forced-march development on the East. And thirdly there was the national mould into which these revolts were somehow inevitably flowing—the new salience of the ethnic, or (as in Bosnia) of the ethnic-religious in post-communist society.[47]

Bourgeois democracies, capitalist economies, nation states—these are the components of our future, according to Nairn. He implies that anyone who objects to the disastrous imposition of multinational capitalism in Russia since 1991 is seeking a return to the genocidal certainties of the Cold War, as if these were the only alternatives facing humanity. In fact, the revolt against the market has already begun in Russia with a 'new development' in the class struggle: 'co-ordination of strike activity across international borders'. The Russian miners, for example, delayed taking strike action in 1996 until it could be co-ordinated with action by miners in the Ukraine.[48]

The impossibility of internationalism?

For Nairn, nationalism is so rooted in our species-being that attempts to displace it in the name of international working class solidarity are misguided. Thus, 'An authentic Internationale can only be based upon the liberation of human nature: which means (in the first instance) nationalities, the precondition for democracy and individual emancipation...'[49] As with his definition of the state, Nairn's own definition of internationalism is classically liberal: 'Internationalism, understood as a systematic outward-looking and inquiring attitude, an imaginative search into the meaning of other experiences, is the most valuable way of counteracting the disadvantages of this truth [that most people live in 'backyards']'.[50] Now, even if I accepted the notion that discrete national cultures exist (which I do not), the outcome desired by Nairn would still be serial nationalism, rather than internationalism. This conclusion in fact predates Nairn's final break with Marxism, and is argued most clearly in 'Internationalism: A Critique'.

He begins by distinguishing between 'internationality' and 'internationalism'. Internationality is the objective result of a capitalist world market in which the same social classes increasingly wear the same clothes, watch the same television programmes and consume the same food and drink, no matter where they are geographically situated. Economic and cultural integration has not, however, led to an identification of political interests between these people, even those which belong to the same social classes. Instead, they have tended to identify with their particular nation, which ultimately involves supporting the state which rules over it. With this much we can agree. The conclusion which Nairn draws, however, is that internationalism is therefore an ideology which, in both Marxist and liberal variants, sets out an essentially moral agenda for overcoming the dominance of nationalism: 'Internationalism poses a moral alternative to the way in which the world has actually gone since the Franco-Prussian War, the end of the First International and, more emphatically, since 1914'.[51]

The reference to 1914 is significant. The collapse of the Second International was a defining moment for Nairn, but not because it demonstrated the betrayal of the international working class movement: 'There was neither betrayal nor regression in this sense'.[52] On the contrary, Nairn argues the socialist parties simply recognised the reality of working class nationalism. Working classes are, at the moment of their initial formation, spontaneously internationalist and anti-capitalist; but this lasts only as long as it takes for them to become integrated into the system, with their own trade unions, co-operatives and political parties— a stage which had been realised in Europe long before 1914.[53] Unable to accept the reality of the situation, however, Marxists retreated into an essentially religious adherence to the internationalist faith, which prevents them responding to the actual—and invariably national—crisis situations which do arise.

Ultimately, conforming to the doctrine of internationalism led socialists into one of two dead ends, whether they were Stalinists or anti-Stalinists: 'The former usurped internationalism into the service of the Soviet Great Russian state, ultimately in still more theocratic terms; the latter responded to this and the other betrayals of the revolution either with distance and pessimism (like some Western Marxists) or with even greater idealisation of the international ideal.' Internationalism for Nairn has therefore essentially been maintained by socialist intellectuals as compensation for the defeats which have dogged the movement since 1917: 'As all-the-samism it is a standing invitation to the notion that "I" (the subject of international revolution, not the unshaven native of Aberdeen or Neusiedle-an-See) am better engaged supporting the revolution where it happens to be at, rather than where I (unshaven native) happen to be located'.[54] But even this is no solution, for these distant revolutions have tended to be driven precisely by the nationalism which the subjects of international revolution oppose: 'To put it crudely—what orthodoxy required was a plausible way of supporting and not supporting national movements at the same time.' Lenin provided the theoretical solution to this conundrum: 'Hence the general principle that all nationalist struggles and movements are bad; however, special and pragmatically identifiable circumstances may make them good—though only for a time, and in a highly qualified fashion.' Thus socialists are free to support national movements until they come to power, then denounce them for refusing to conform to the internationalist ideal: 'Each new tragedy of Balkanisation serves to underlie the ever fresh principle that only the international class struggle can prevent this kind of thing—if only the revisionist and narrow nationalists can be stopped, next time.' The alternative to this, Nairn argues, would be the psychologically impossible one of admitting the inevitability of nationalism.

Marxists are therefore taxed with refusing to recognise the power of nationalism, with adhering to an illusionary theory of internationalism, and hypocritically supporting national movements (as 'exceptions') in the inevitable absence of that internationalism. There is, however, one final indictment to be added to the charge sheet. As Alex Callinicos has written, 'It has become part of the common sense beliefs of large sectors of the Western intelligentsia that every universalism is a masked particularism'.[55] For Nairn, the universalism of internationalism disguises a particularism of big battalion nationalism, such as that displayed by socialists who opposed Scottish self-determination in favour of the British state, or, for that matter, those who opposed self-determination for Azerbeijan in favour of the old USSR.

Part 2: The reality of nationalism—capitalism and reformism

I have given Nairn the benefit of an extended presentation of his position, delivered as far as possible in his own words. I now want to examine the relationship of nationalism respectively to modernity, capitalism, reformism and internationalism, before returning to engage with Nairn's current position on Scotland.

i) Nationalism as an aspect of modernity. According to Anthony Smith, there are three basic positions on the place of nations and nationalism in historical development. The first, appropriately enough, is primordialism: 'proponents of this view claim that nations and ethnic communities are the natural units of history and integral elements of human experience...[the] basic organising principles and bonds of human association throughout history.' The second is perennialism, whose advocates argue that 'units and sentiments found in the modern world are simply larger and more effective units and sentiments traceable in much earlier periods of human history'. The third and final position is modernism, where:

...the nation is a purely modern phenomenon, a product of strictly modern developments like capitalism, bureaucracy and secular utilitarianism... Nations and nationalism, the argument continues, can be dated with some precision to the latter half of the 18th century...anything which appears to

resemble it, either in antiquity or the Middle Ages must be understood as purely fortuitous or exceptional.[56]

The modernist position (once held by Nairn) refuses all attempts to claim that nationalism is an inescapable part of the human condition. As the late Ernest Gellner wrote, the primordialist theory is the most commonly invoked of the three, but 'in one sense it is barely a theory, because it treats the principle as something inherent in human nature, or the very principles of social organisation, so obvious as not really to require explanation.' If anyone points out that for the most of human existence this aspect of our nature has been absent, nationalists have an answer:

Nationalists are in fact aware of the evidence which makes some of us contest the universality of nationalist sentiments: they do know, often with anger, that in many societies and many historical periods, nationalism is conspicuous by its absence. They know it, with great bitterness, especially when it relates to the recent past of their own nation. But they explain it in their own way, and their explanation is contained in what is probably the most commonly used word in the nationalist vocabulary: awakening.[57]

Nairn is aware of Gellner's critique,[58] yet the notion of 'awakening' is the basis of his explanation for the revival of Scottish nationalism and indeed of all other nationalisms. The reader may have already noted his use of the term in passing—'As far as the "bourgeois" aspects of the 1970s national movement are concerned, I remain convinced that in our specific conditions only the middle strata could have brought about such an awakening'—but now we learn that 'the Treaty of Union came just in time to bury a nascent Scottish nationalism, but could only put it into a shallow grave.' And from this grave, 'The corpse may simply step out from temporary interment to claim his rights'.[59] In a sense this goes one better than Gellner: not only an awakening but a veritable second coming. We will examine the Lazarus of European nationalisms at the conclusion of this article. For the moment, however, let us stick with the question of modernity.

Those who accept that nationalism is a modern phenomenon tend to uphold one of two main theoretical approaches. On the one hand, followers of the German sociologist Max Weber argue that nations are a product of the process which they call modernisation, particularly during the phase involving industrialisation. On the other, Marxists argue that these terms ignore the fact that 'modernising' societies have been subject to a much more specific process: domination by the capitalist mode of production. It was the first of these approaches, embodied in the work of Ernest Gellner, which influenced Nairn in his original reflections on the national question, but Nairn avoided the issue by treating modernity and capitalism as equivalent.[60]

Since Nairn now treats nationalism as a permanent aspect of the human condition, he has consequently dissociated it from both modernisation *and* the capitalist mode of production (although, as we have seen, he is happy to use the notion of a transition from 'traditional' to 'modern' societies as an explanation for nationalisms of which he disapproves).

ii) Nationalism and capitalism. Once a nation state has been established, those who control the state apparatus always seek to consolidate the hold of 'national consciousness' among the people who inhabit the state territory. As Nigel Harris puts it, 'Once the boundary is beaten back and troops posted around the perimeter, the state undertakes to colonise all within, to drill all the inhabitants who find themselves trapped behind the fence with an invented common inheritance of loyalty, supposedly to a common culture or way of life, but in practice to a particular state.'[61] This certainly happens, although Nairn is largely silent on the issue, but the suggestion that nationalism exists purely as the result of indoctrination is hardly the whole explanation. Why do workers support nationalist movements before states are established? Why do they accept it afterwards? One reason is clearly that bourgeois ideology is at its most convincing when it appears to confirm the inevitably of the world as it is organised under capitalism, which is one consisting of actual or potential nation states. There is, however, another reason. Nairn is correct to suggest that nationalism provides a framework of identity, a sense of 'belonging'; the question is whether it is the only form of consciousness which can play this role.

Benedict Anderson once suggested that the origins of national consciousness lay in the collapse of 'three fundamental cultural conceptions' during the rise of capitalism: the identification of 'a particular script-language' (such as Latin in Christendom) with access to religious truth; the belief that society was organised in a natural hierarchy, at the summit of which were 'monarchs who were persons apart from other human beings'; and a view of the indistinguishability of cosmology and history which rendered 'the origins of the world and of men essentially identical'. The interconnected decline of these three meant that human beings required 'a new way of linking fraternity, power and time meaningfully together'.[62] As Chris Harman has noted, this argument makes the connection of nationalism with capitalist development contingent rather than necessary, with the latter simply allowing expression to an 'existential yearning', providing an outlet for 'the satisfaction of innate psychological needs'.[63] It is, however, possible to reformulate the position held by Anderson in a way which relies not on a conception of the eternal human condition—which would be to surrender to the position held by Nairn—but on the human needs which are created by capitalism.[64]

As George Kerevan once wrote, ironically in Nairn's journal, *The Bulletin Of Scottish Politics*:

> *If civil society separates itself from people's social-political designation (as opposed to their party-political designation); if individuals only face one another in the market connected in only one all-embracing unit of civil society—the nation... A mass social allegiance is born; an allegiance to something beyond the class antagonisms of civil society, beyond language, beyond ethnicity, beyond geography: nationalism. For the feudal peasant, whose unfreedom is not masked by the market, no such allegiance is possible.*

For workers under capitalism, however, such an allegiance is not only possible, it is—from the point of view of the capitalist class in individual nations—absolutely necessary; for without it, the danger is always that workers will identify not with the nation in which they happen to be situated, but with the class to which they are condemned to belong, regardless of the accident of geographical location. Consequently, as Kerevan points out, workers are confronted by 'two materially conditioned allegiances'. On the one hand, '*Nationalism*, reflecting the social position of the individual caught in the allegiances imposed by civil society and its exterior state.' On the other, '*Proletarian internationalism*, reflecting the class position of the worker and the kernel of the socialist mode of production developing within capitalism.' The two are quite different in nature: 'The former is materially determined by the external appearance of bourgeois society, the latter by its essence'.[65]

iii) *Nationalism and reformism*. Nationalism should not therefore be seen as something which only 'happens' during separatist movements on the one hand, or during fascist and imperialist manifestations on the other. The capitalist system generates nationalism as a necessary, everyday condition of its existence. Consequently, it forms part of the reformist consciousness among the working class. Reformism, long before it becomes embodied in organisation, is produced by the tension between accepting the system as a unchanging feature of human life, and rejecting the way in which specific aspects of it actually impact on our lives. The task for revolutionaries is, as it were, to expand this 'rejectionist' side of reformist consciousness until it becomes total, proving through a combination of argument and activity that, for example, the inadequacy of our schools is neither accidental nor incidental, but a direct effect of how the system operates.

The difficulty is that reformist political organisations are constantly pulling in the opposite direction, reinforcing nationalism at the same time as they encourage workers to accept the system. This is for two reasons. The first is the well known tendency of reformist parties to appeal to the lowest levels of working class consciousness, rather than attempt to raise them; to pander to the worst forms of working class prejudice rather than attempt to challenge it. The second is that these reformists hope to take over national government office themselves—despite all the talk of globalisation, the assumption is still that the national state is the arena in which 'politics' is conducted. Nairn therefore completely underestimates (or rather, wilfully disregards) the extent to which the reformist and Stalinist left have been responsible for the continued dominance of nationalist consciousness among the working class under capitalism.[66] Rather than having no alternative but to reflect an overwhelming nationalist feeling among the working class, they consciously attempt to foster these feelings.[67] Within the trade unions this can occur in two ways, both of which can be illustrated from the experience of the labour movement in Scotland.

The first is the argument that particular industries or workplaces belong to 'the nation', rather than to capitalist firms or (more rarely these days) the capitalist state. The disastrous effects of this ideology became apparent during the Miners' Strike of 1984-1985.[68] One of the key objectives of the NUM was to stop steel production nationally. Unfortunately the leadership relied on their fellow officials in the steel unions delivering this rather than picketing out the steel workers. The latter had been badly defeated in the steel strike of 1980 and more than half the workforce had been lost in the ensuing three years. The leadership of the Iron and Steel Trades Confederation opposed shutting down steel production.

It was at this point that the Scottish nationalist argument kicked in. In Scotland, the NUM Area officials signed an agreement allowing enough coal to enter the strip mill at Ravenscraig in Motherwell to keep the furnaces operating. The reason given by Area President Mick McGahey was that the deal was 'in the interests of Scotland's industrial future'. In fact, not only did the amount of coal entering Ravenscraig not drop from its normal levels to that required on a care-and-maintenance basis, it *increased*. Picketing by the miners and their supporters was unable to close the plant in the absence of practical solidarity from other unions or the STUC. And so the 'Scottish national interest' helped play its part in the defeat of the NUM, the destruction of the British mining industry and the perpetuation of Tory rule for another 12 years.

Pursuit of the national interest also left a legacy of division within the Scottish working class which should not be underestimated. Joe Owens, a miner who worked at Polkemmet Colliery in East Lothian before the strike, gave vent to his feelings in an interview several years later:

> *And when the miners asked the men at Ravenscraig not to accept imported coal, they just put two fingers up at them, which was another contributing factor to the closure of Polkemmet.* Since that event, of course, Ravenscraig has been closed and they're looking for everybody's sympathy after turning down the miners' appeals. I've no sympathy for them, same as I've none for the Nottinghamshire miners [ie who formed the scab Union of Democratic Mineworkers during the strike]. I'm actually praying for pits to close in Nottingham so that I can laugh at them.[69]

The second way in which nationalism is fostered by the reformist bureaucracy is in the advocacy of all-class, pan-Scottish alliance as the way to defend jobs. Despite the comments quoted above, delegates at the Scottish NUM conference in June 1990 voted to support the campaign to save Ravenscraig from closure, and union convener Tommy Brennan was even invited to speak at the annual Miners' Gala in Edinburgh. But this was simply the latest in a series of campaigns which had followed the same disastrous course over every threatened closure since the Upper Clyde Shipbuilders' work-in of 1971. The composition of these coalitions, invariably led by the Scottish TUC, was summarised by one friendly critic as consisting of 'trade unionists, clergymen, artists, politicians of various hue [ie they included Tories], thinkers, councillors, professionals, and the rest'.[70] They inevitably refused to consider industrial action and focused instead on 'mobilising Scottish public opinion' on the one hand (unnecessarily, since in most cases it was already in sympathy with the threatened workers) and attempting to 'persuade' the government to intervene (pointlessly, since it was usually in complete agreement with the employers). Of these campaigns, only the first at Upper Clyde Shipbuilders achieved any kind of success, and that because it was accompanied by a militant occupation which took place in the context of the great upturn in British working class struggle of the early 1970s. The others—Singer at Clydebank, the Carron Iron Works, British Leyland at Bathgate, the Corpach paper mill, the Invergordon smelter, Linwood, Caterpillar, Ravenscraig—took place in a period of defeat and contributed to extending it by their failure. As Keith Aitken writes:

> *Retrospection yields the dispiriting, and somehow surprising, realisation that almost none of the eighties issue coalitions achieved their primary objectives. They did not save Caterpillar or Ravenscraig. They did not change government policy on health, devolution or the economy.*[71]

It was not until the Timex workers in Dundee fought back in 1993 that this strategy was effectively challenged, and not until the victory of the Glacier RPB workers in Glasgow during 1996 that the cycle of disaster was broken, although there is no sign that the STUC have learned any lessons from the experience. And there can be little doubt that in an independent Scotland there will be increased reformist pressure on workers, both to identify with 'their' capitalism against that of other rival nations, and to unite with other social classes in Scotland to 'solve' the local manifestations of the global crisis. The point is that what Nairn identifies as the dominance of nationalism within the working class is to a large extent the dominance of reformism, of which nationalism is a necessary component. But if nationalism in this sense is part of reformist consciousness then it can be challenged in exactly the same way as reformism can in every other sphere of life. Indeed, one might say that workers remain attached to nationalist loyalties to the extent that they remain subject to reformist consciousness.

iv) Nationalism and internationalism. Internationalism is as much a component of revolutionary consciousness and politics as nationalism is of reformist consciousness and politics. It has two aspects. On the one hand, it involves workers in one nation giving solidarity to workers in other nations, even at a cost to themselves: for example, the support given to the Liverpool dockers from as far afield as the United States and Australia. Here the issue is the unity of working class interests against employers or the state, regardless of national boundaries. On the other hand, internationalism also involves workers in one nation giving solidarity to the national aspirations of the people of another nation, who will—by definition—include non-workers and are usually led by quite alien class forces: for example, the opposition mounted in both Britain and the US to the bombing of Iraq.

A small but illuminating example of both aspects—solidarity with both a working class and a nation—was once given, appropriately enough, in Nairn's native region of Fife. In 1974, a year after the military coup in Chile, the Chilean submarine *O'Brien* docked in Greenock in order that tailshafts could be repaired, protected and then sent back to South America as spares. When the tailshafts arrived at the Royal Navy dockyard at Rosyth the TGWU shop stewards in the stores organisation refused to release them and wrote to the Ministry of Defence informing it 'that no future Chilean Navy work will be done in Rosyth dockyard until the fascist *junta* is removed and a freely, democratically elected government put in power and human rights restored in Chile'. The blacking went on for four years until the MOD eventually agreed that no work would be carried out or supplies provided to the *junta* by that dockyard. Rosyth was not traditionally a militant workplace; it had participated in the 'Hands Off Russia' agitation in 1919, but in that case the driving force had been a group of Portsmouth engineers temporarily based in Fife. In 1974 the catalyst for action was a group of left wing stewards who were active locally in the Labour Party, demonstrating that where internationalist arguments are consistently put, they can influence the actions of workers.[72]

Internationalism is not simply a moral imperative which workers can respond to or not, according to inclination, but a practical necessity given the nature of the capitalist order. The Fife shipyard workers referred to above may not have been immediately threatened by a military dictatorship, but they understood that the ease or difficulty with which the *junta* was able to go about its business in the world would have a bearing on whether other ruling classes were inclined to go down the road to repression. Furthermore, it is a necessity which the interconnectedness of the system—its 'internationality', to use Nairn's phrase—makes possible because it is not simply a question of the clothes people wear or the television programmes they watch, but a shared relationship to the reproduction of an international system. At a trade union level, the support shown by the Australian maritime union to the Liverpool dockers was at least partly a recognition that their own employers were planning a similar onslaught—which eventually came within weeks of the dispute coming to an end.[73] It is also true that the cultural aspects of 'internationality', notably the growth of a global media, have simply made people more aware of the similarity between their struggles and those happening in other parts of the world.

I want, however, to dwell briefly on the second aspect of internationalism, since it is one of the biggest sources of confusion, not least to Nairn, who persistently mistakes the effect of Stalinism (including the effect it has had on 'orthodox' Trotskyism) and the ideological rubbish left in its wake for the genuine Marxist position. It is important to state first of all that there is no metaphysical 'right of nations to self-determination' (the unfortunate title of Lenin's otherwise indispensable pamphlet notwithstanding). Nor, contrary to what Nairn asserts, has the Marxist position ever been to support 'exceptional' or 'good' nationalisms. Socialists never support *nationalism* but they do support specific *national demands* under certain conditions. What are these?

This question is often reduced to the attitude taken by Marxists to oppressed peoples struggling against imperialism and its local agents— understandably, since for more than the first half of this century this issue largely *was* 'the national question'. The basis of socialist support for these nationalist movements was set out in the debates at the first four Congresses of the Communist International; the rise to full human dignity of peoples who had previously been regarded (and in some cases regarded themselves) as naturally inferior to their colonial masters, the weakening effect which national revolts had on the world system as a whole, the opportunity which they gave for socialists to break workers in the West from racism and support for imperialism and, consequently, to demonstrate to the colonial peoples that Western workers supported them rather than their 'own' capitalists or state. None of this meant supporting the politics of the national movements themselves. Not the least distorting effect of Stalinism was to convince the majority of the international left that these national movements were socialist in content (so that when the true nature of, say, the Vietnamese regime was exposed it contributed to disillusion with the very idea of socialism). Since the end of Stalinism this view has nevertheless remained alive, but in the form of arguing that in every situation there must be one national movement which is oppressed and deserves support.

For socialists, however, the question of support for particular national demands (not for particular nationalisms) is determined by their relationship to the struggle for socialism, regardless of whether the nation concerned is oppressed or not. Furthermore, it should openly be undertaken with the purpose of weakening the support of workers for that nationalism. In this context several questions have to asked. Does support strengthen or weaken the capitalist or imperialist state? Does support strengthen or weaken the class consciousness and organisation of the working class? Does support strengthen or weaken the tolerance of people of different nations or 'races' for each other? These are not always easy questions to answer, particularly where (as in Scotland) no element of national oppression is involved. Nevertheless, to try and answer them seems preferable to conceding in advance both the legitimacy of every nationalism and our inability to make any value judgements between them.

Politics and the modern Lazarus

The previous paragraph brought us back to Scotland, our starting point. Let us examine Nairn's current views on this subject, then conclude. First, we need to understand his assessment of contemporary Scottish nationalism. According to Nairn, the political nationalism which arose in the 1960s 'was not solely a wish for exit from the United Kingdom: it was, in effect, the desire to escape from "civil society" and resume business as a political society' in his native Scotland, where, we learn, 'a "civil" social order (with the sense of "decency", privacy, individual and group minority rights, *freedom of initiative and enterprise*, etc) depends in the long run upon an appropriately civil form of national identity'.[74] From this perspective, 'civil society' is merely 'a fall-back position for middle class internationalists' opposed to Scottish nationalism.[75] It should not be thought, however, that Nairn is opposed to the middle class as such; on the contrary, they must be at the heart of the Scottish nationalist project.

In fact, at one level, Nairn is far more honest about the class basis of Scottish nationalism than the SNP could ever be: 'Though led in the name of a indeterminate "people", national liberation struggle can only be led by certain people with more determinate and vested interests in the process; nor could it conceivably be otherwise.' And who is this class in Scotland? According to Nairn, it is the one which 'runs Scotland—the institutional middle class', with which he identifies himself as a 'recalcitrant member': 'No collective presumption is intended here, for the important term is "runs": the Scottish institutional middle class has never ruled this country, it merely manages it'.[76] Actually, no middle class—institutional or not—has ever ruled any country, the bourgeoisie does that. For Nairn, however, failure to win the support of the former group was at the root of the SNP's inability to make an electoral breakthrough: 'In this sense, perhaps, the SNP version of national identity has never been half "bourgeois" enough—it was a twopenny solution aimed at a bit of everyone and no one in particular.' However, the Scottish middle class was now beginning to take its national identity seriously under 'the lash of Thatcherism'.[77]

Now, there is a sense in which this is absolutely correct. The original class basis for the SNP during the 1960s and 1970s was the old petty bourgeoisie, 'the small man, the frustrated Scottish businessman smelling profit in oil yet unable to cash in, only to spectate, and the lower middle class and professional elements watching their hard non-status and security disappear in the furnace of inflation'.[78] There is no doubt that elements of the new middle class are now dominant within the SNP, their presence symbolised by the leadership of former Bank of Scotland economist Alex Salmond. The important fact here, however, is that the working class has not been won over to political nationalism, a fact of which Nairn is no doubt aware, but which has no great significance for him precisely because he now regards working class politics as irrelevant. For revolutionaries, however, it is crucial. Yet the failure of Scottish nationalism in this respect is often unappreciated both inside and outside Scotland, largely as a result of misinterpreting two kinds of opinion poll.

The first are those which show a growing tendency for respondents to claim that they feel more Scottish than British (33 percent in June 1998 compared to 29 percent in September 1991).[79] Yet this indicates an increase in national consciousness, not nationalism as such, although the former is a necessary precondition of the latter. This consciousness has been shared, since the latter half of the 18th century, with a sense of Britishness, but assertion of the Scottish 'side' of this dual identity has no necessary political implications. As Joyce McMillan once noted, 'Scottish identity requires constant assertion, whereas British identity is something taken for granted by every institution with which [the Scots] have to deal, and inclined to assert itself in the half conscious assumption that politics is something that happens at Westminster'.[80]

The point here is not that there is anything desirable about feeling British rather than Scottish or any other nationality but rather that, precisely because political and economic issues have tended to be resolved at a British level, that side of the national identity is where class unity is usually expressed. Britishness tends to be assumed at some level by all classes in Scotland (the same poll cited above shows that only 28 percent of Scots do not feel British to any degree). A genuine hardening of Scottish consciousness into a political nationalism, precisely because its goal would be to establish a new state, would necessarily be accompanied by an emphasis on the unity of all Scots against that of British workers.

The second set of polls show a growing tendency for Scots to say that they would vote for independence in a referendum about the constitutional future and vote for the SNP in the Scottish Parliament: the most recent shows 56 percent opting for the former and 40 percent for latter— the same percentage as those saying they would vote for Labour.[81] What these results both demonstrate is not some asocial upsurge of primeval nationalism, but a response to the actions of the Blair government. The SNP made few advances in working class areas at the general election of 1997. Despite posturing as the inheritor of Labour's social democratic past it gained only two Tory seats in predominantly rural areas. Yet after the hopes of 1 May 1997 were dashed, the SNP provides an electorally credible and seemingly left wing alternative for Scottish voters of a type which is not (and cannot be) available in England. The SNP is not a reformist party like Labour, but we are dealing here with perception, not reality.[82]

Two other points of interest arising from these polls deserve to be mentioned. First, that the numbers claiming to favour independence for Scotland exceed by 16 percent those claiming they would vote for the SNP, which suggests that independence as means of achieving certain political objectives and Scottish nationalism as a set of political beliefs are not necessarily seen as linked. Secondly, these are voting intentions for the Scottish Parliament, not Westminster, where the SNP has consistently failed to achieve levels of Labour support, which suggests that voting for the SNP might be seen as a luxury which can be indulged without the threat of doing too much damage.

The establishment of a Scottish Parliament was, after the election of a Labour government, the solution most commonly offered by reformists to problems of the working class in Scotland during the years of Tory rule. Given the nature of the current Labour government, it comes as no surprise that those who are anxious to take the path of least resistance have focused still more on what the parliament will deliver. Does Nairn share these illusions? Here we return full circle to the question of the British state. Nairn so loathes the aged beast that his reaction to the Labour victory on 1 May 1997 was very restrained.[83] Nairn correctly saw that Blair would do nothing to disturb the existing set-up, unless forced to, but completely misunderstands what lay behind the vote for a parliament with 'tax varying' powers on 13 September 1997: 'The most important thing for a recalled Parliament to decide, I need hardly point out, is not raising or lowering income tax by a few percent. It will be whether to alter the conditions of UK affiliation'.[84]

Nairn now seems confident that this will happen. In a speech to the annual conference of the Centre of Research into Elections and Social Trends during November 1997 he foresaw that: 'Within the crumbling clam-shell of British sovereignty, serious home rule...will find it hard to avoid *de facto* sovereignty'.[85] There are two issues here.

First, what is sovereignty for, exactly? This obsession with sovereignty for its own sake (taking into account Nairn's concern to protect 'enterprise') is about the most right wing position available within the pan-nationalist camp.

Secondly, are the 'conditions of UK affiliation' the central issue for most Scots? The 1997 Scottish Election Survey found that 54 percent of respondents expected 'the economy' to be better after the establishment of a Scottish Parliament (13 percent by 'a lot', 41 percent by 'a little'), 38 percent expected unemployment to be better (6 percent and 32 percent), 62 percent expected education to be better (17 percent and 45 percent) and 60 percent expected the NHS to be better (16 percent and 44 percent).[86] These findings tend to suggest two conclusions. One is that the main reasons why people want a Scottish Parliament are immediate social issues, not abstractions about sovereignty. The other is that, even so, they do not expect it to make more than marginal improvements to the quality of their lives. Nairn, on the other hand, believes that a Scottish polity will somehow be innately beneficent. Writing of the anti Poll Tax campaign he notes that: 'Everyone there... knew perfectly well that no Scottish legislation would ever conceivably have imposed such a tax to begin with'.[87] As is well known, the powers enjoyed by the parliament will be extremely limited, although opportunities will exist for agitation and propaganda around issues like education where it does have some control. The voting system for the elections of May 1999 has been deliberately devised to prevent as far as possible any individuals or organisations from outside the established parties getting elected. Furthermore, it is likely to produce a coalition politics in which both Labour and the SNP will be able to claim that they are unable to carry out radical policies because of the need to placate their coalition partners, whoever they are. Finally, the process by which the Labour candidates has been selected has eliminated all but a few token left wingers in favour of faithful Blairites. On the whole, the prospects of the Scottish Parliament producing something as offensive as the Poll Tax are probably rather high.

Nairn is obviously aware of all this, but probably thinks that an increase in power for the parliament is inevitable, its very existence leading a heightened desire for more 'sovereignty'. But this in turn is predicated on the false belief that 'sovereignty' is a matter of importance to the majority of Scots. What most working class Scots want is the control over their lives and conditions that no bourgeois parliament in Westminster or Holyrood can give them—the control which bourgeois parliaments are in fact specifically designed to prevent working class people achieving. When it becomes apparent that the Scottish Parliament will not live up to even the minimum expectations invested in it, then a number of responses are possible. One might be the outcome desired by Nairn (and in a more directly electoral way by the SNP), where parliamentary failure is seen as stemming from the absence of Scottish sovereignty and leads to the demand for independent nationhood becoming irresistible. Another might be that failure condemns it to irrelevance, and instead of provoking high levels of public interest it becomes the object of the same sort of bemused contempt with which local authorities are currently viewed. Still another might be that its failures are seen, not as the result of a lack of independence, but because it is a reformist institution incapable of challenging capitalism in Scotland or anywhere else. The latter perception is, of course, correct and the one which revolutionaries will seek to make hegemonic among the working class. If we fail, it will be for political reasons, not because our audience was genetically predisposed to embrace nationalism.

One final point is worth considering. Nairn always tended to treat the British state as if it had a life of its own, apart from the class interests which it represents. His argument nevertheless assumed that 'the break-up of Britain' would represent a defeat for the British ruling class, and that it would oppose the departure of Scotland—indeed, this was one of the very reasons why the idea of Scottish independence had such a resonance on the left. It is by no means certain, however, that the British ruling class will necessarily remain committed to the preservation of the British state in its current form, if it can be demonstrated that other constitutional arrangements will equally serve their interests to the same extent. As early as 1990, *The Economist*, playing its usual role as outrider for the most extreme doctrines of free market ideology, suggested in a leader article that there might be advantages in Scotland achieving independence: 'Unable to rely on handouts from the British exchequer, Scotland's political classes would take unpopular closure decisions for themselves, or leave managers free to do so.' The editorial looked forward to 'the replacement of today's half angry, half embarrassed dependency status by a grown up political culture', capable of closing down plants like Ravenscraig without concession to 'industrial romanticism'.[88]

This was a lone voice at the time, but there are signs that the bourgeoisie themselves—and not just their ideologists—might now be prepared to contemplate full independence, not on free market doctrinal grounds, but as part of the search for stability. The *Financial Times* reported recently that 'what worries business is the prospect of endless uncertainty and altercation over Scotland's status, rather than the nature of the eventual settlement'.[89] The declining Scottish economy is unlikely to reproduce the relative success of Catalonian devolution. The prospect of the national question becoming a permanent feature of Scottish politics, as it has become in Quebec, would therefore make independence attractive simply because it would decide the issue once and for all. This is a view which may gather strength once the parliament is established. At the moment, much more typical is Andrew Neil's talk of creating a 'new Unionism…within a much more devolved, even federalist, United Kingdom', but Neil—once accurately described by Nairn as an 'archetypal Scotch crawler'—will ultimately be less important in deciding the path of the British state than the capitalists he admires so much.[90] If Scottish independence does become something that the British capitalist class can live with, then one of the key arguments on the left for supporting it—that it is against the interests of the bourgeoisie—will have effectively dissolved. One of the tragedies of Nairn's trajectory towards the acceptance of 'enterprise' is that this is no longer even an issue for him.

'We are all German Jews'

In one of the essays in *Faces Of Nationalism*, Nairn reviews *The Race Gallery*, by Marek Kohn, from which he extracts two morals. The first is that 'Human biological diversity needs to be explored not denied.' And the second is that 'diversity needs some new defences in order to survive'. The reader will have no difficulty in guessing what the nature of these new defences are likely to be. Nairn is thinking here in particular of the Roma population of East Central Europe, who have suffered renewed levels of racism since the fall of Stalinism. Needless to say, as far as Nairn is concerned there is no possibility that this can be resisted; the Roma must simply establish their own nationalism in opposition which will 'inevitably' be 'ethno-linguistic or "racial".'[91]

The tragedy of Nairn's long retreat from Marxism is that for one brief moment he did recognise, in all its grandeur, the possibilities for socialist revolution, not as a myth, but as an actuality which provided the solution to racial and national oppression:

> *When de Gaulle spoke with condescension of 'the new blood of France', to be* *'given a voice' after May, he revealed only his own ignorance of a generation* *that had spewed out that 'France' along with the priests, professors and* *policemen, and adopted 'Nous sommes tous des Juifs-Allemands' as its* *motto, doing more for the cause of internationalism and European unity in* *one day than the governments and labour bureaucracies of Western Europe* *had achieved in twenty years.*[92]

'Nous sommes tous des Juifs-Allemands'—'We are all German Jews'—was the slogan of the French students and workers who demonstrated in May 1968 after attacks on Daniel Cohn-Bendit as a 'German Jew' in the bourgeois press had led to his attempted assassination. Nairn could once use the very same slogan against the paltry vision offered to Scotland by nationalism: 'To acquiesce in the SNP's version of our future, in the year where a new generation cried "Nous sommes tous des Juifs-Allemands" before the Palais Bourbon and ground the nationalism of the past to dust at the Saarbrucken bridge, is merely an uninteresting form of suicide'.[93] It seems likely that when another new generation arises to proclaim themselves German Jews (or perhaps Punjabi Scots), Nairn will now be one of those pressing the hemlock into our hands. 'A false political theory bears within itself its own punishment', wrote Trotsky in 1933.[94] There is no need for the working class in Scotland or anywhere else to suffer that punishment, but one prerequisite for escaping it is precisely to see ourselves primarily as workers, and to reject all theories which would have us believe that the accidental fact of Scottish nationhood, or any other, is what will determine our fate.

Notes

Many thanks to Alex Law.

1   Excluding *The Break-Up of Britain* itself, the major works in order of appearance
     are: H Seton-Watson, *Nations And States* (London, 1977); J Breuilly, *Nationalism*
     And The State (Manchester, 1982 and 1993); E Gellner, *Nations And Nationalism*
     (Oxford, 1983); B Anderson, *Imagined Communities* (London and New York,

1983 and 1991); A D Smith, *The Ethnic Origins Of Nations* (Oxford, 1986); E J Hobsbawm, *Nations And Nationalism Since 1780* (Cambridge, 1990); N Harris, *National Liberation* (London and New York, 1990); A D Smith, *National Identity* (Harmondsworth, 1991); L Greenfield, *Nationalism* (London, 1992); and E Gellner, *Nationalism* (London, 1997). The books by Anderson, Harris, Hobsbawm and the first by Gellner are reviewed in C Harman, 'The Return of the National Question', *International Socialism* 56, Autumn 1992, pp4, 41-49.

2   T Nairn, 'The Modern Janus', *New Left Review* 94, November-December 1975, p3; *The Break-Up of Britain*, p329.

3   For an example of the first, see N Gentchev, 'Lambs to the Slaughter?', *Socialist Review* 218, April 1998, pp29-30; for an example of the second, see I Bell 'Spirit of nationhood alive and kicking as the world goes global', *The Scotsman*, 9 February 1998.

4   The point was made long ago by James Kellas: 'The fortunes of the SNP have of course affected the intensity of national consciousness, but such consciousness is greater than the number of votes won by that party at elections. It is not necessarily concerned, as is the SNP with "national self determination", or with political devolution. It is rather an expression of Scottishness on the part of an amorphous group of interests and individuals, whose identity is caught up with that of Scotland.' J G Kellas, *The Scottish Political System* (Second Edition, Cambridge, 1975), p119.

5   T Nairn, 'The Question of Scotland', *Faces of Nationalism*, p189.

6   W Thompson, 'Tom Nairn and the Crisis of the British State', *Contemporary Record*, 6:2, Autumn 1992, p308. This interesting, if over-reverential, article is based in part on an interview with Nairn conducted on 17 December 1991 and is a useful source of information about his career. See also P Anderson, 'Foreword', *English Questions* (London and New York, 1992), p3.

7   T Nairn, 'The Twilight of the British State' *New Left Review* 101-102, February-April 1977, p49; *The Break-Up of Britain*, p75.

8   L D Trotsky, *The History Of The Russian Revolution* (London, 1977), p27; 'Where Is Britain Going?', *Collected Writings And Speeches On Britain* (3 Volumes, London, 1974), vol 2, pp14, 39-40.

9   A Callinicos, 'Exception or Symptom? The British Crisis and the World System', *New Left Review* 169, May-June 1988, p103.

10   The literature on the 'Nairn-Anderson thesis' is too vast to be listed here. Virtually the only contribution to the debate to treat Nairn as seriously as it did Anderson was the first, E P Thompson's 'The Peculiarities of the English' (1965). This great (and extremely funny) essay is best savoured in the complete version published in *The Poverty Of Theory And Other Essays* (London, 1978). A brief but pointed critique of the 'thesis' from the perspective of this journal can be found in A Callinicos, op cit. Various misconceptions about working class politics during the 19th century are corrected in C Bambery, 'Myth and Reality in British Working Class Struggle', in J Rees (ed), *Essays On Historical Materialism* (London, 1998), although Bambery takes Anderson rather than Nairn as the starting point for his discussion.

11   J Brand, *The National Movement In Scotland* (London, 1978), pp258-262.

12   T Nairn, 'The Three Dreams of Scottish Nationalism', *New Left Review* 49, May-June 1968, p7.

13   Ibid, p13.

14   Ibid, p16.

15   Ibid, p18.

16   T Nairn, 'The Left Against Europe?', *New Left Review* 75, September-October 1972, pp116-9.

17   T Nairn, 'Scotland and Europe', *New Left Review* 83, January-February 1974, pp63, 60; *The Break-Up of Britain*, pp99, 96.

18   T Nairn, 'Old and New Scottish Nationalism', in G Brown (ed), *The Red Paper On Scotland* (Edinburgh, 1975), pp47, 49; *The Break-Up of Britain*, p179. The majority of the quoted passages were not included in the later version of this essay.

19   Ibid: *The Red Paper On Scotland*, p24; *The Break-Up of Britain*, p130.

20   For an example of the first, see 'Scotland and Europe': 'After the dark, the unspeakable 17th century...it was 1688 which marked the real dawn in Scotland', *The Break-Up of Britain*, p109. For an example of the second, see 'Old and New Scottish Nationalism': '[Kailyard culture] is recognisably intertwined with that prodigious array of Kitsch symbols, slogans, ornaments, banners, war-cries, knick-knacks, music-hall heroes, icons, conventional sayings and sentiments (not a few of them "pithy") which have for so long resolutely defended the name of "Scotland" to the world. Annie Swan and [A J] Cronin provided no more than the relatively decent outer garb for the vast tartan monster. In their work the thing trots along doucely enough, on a lead. But it is something else to be with it (eg) in a London pub on International night, or in the crowd at the annual Military Tattoo in front of Edinburgh Castle. How intolerably vulgar! What unbearable, crass, mindless philistinism! One knows that Kitsch is a large constituent of mass popular culture in every land: but this is ridiculous!' *The Red Paper On Scotland*, p39; *The Break-Up of Britain*, p162. On second thoughts, given the success of *Braveheart*, and the recent announcement that 6 April is henceforth to be celebrated in the US as 'Tartan Day', perhaps Nairn does not exaggerate too grossly after all.

21   C Beveridge and R Turnbull, 'Scottish Nationalist, British Marxist: the Strange Case of Tom Nairn', *The Eclipse Of Scottish Culture* (Edinburgh, 1989), pp59, 60.

22   T Nairn, 'The Twilight of the British State', *New Left Review* 101-102, February-April 1977, pp59-60; *The Break-Up of Britain*, pp89-90.

23   T Nairn, 'The Modern Janus: *New Left Review* 94, pp12, 18, 22-23; *The Break-Up of Britain*, pp339-340, 348-349, 354.

24   T Nairn, 'The National Question', internal SLP document, cited in H Drucker, *Breakaway: the Scottish Labour Party* (Edinburgh, n.d. [1978]), p124.

25   Cartoons of Oor Wullie advancing slogans along the lines of 'Jings! It's not Devolution we need, it's Revolution!' soon followed in *Socialist Worker*. While no doubt formally correct, this was not perhaps the best way to engage the Scottish working class in discussion of the issue.

26   A Marr, *The Battle For Scotland* (Harmondsworth, 1992), p162.

27   T Nairn, *Faces of Nationalism*, p227.

28   E Heffer, *Never A Yes Man* (London and New York, 1991), p165. Heffer records how his views were received in parliament: 'In the Commons I made speeches drawing attention to what the Austro-Marxists and [Rosa] Luxemburg had argued... They cut little ice.' It is part of the tragedy of his political career that he ever imagined they would in this setting.

29   T Nairn, 'Postscript 1981: Into Political Emergency', *The Break-Up of Britain*, pp288, 397-398.

30   See ibid, pp402-404 and, more optimistically, an article called—inevitably—'The Crisis of the British State', *New Left Review* 130, November-December 1981, pp41-44. As Perry Anderson once pointed out, words, like currency, lose value through inflation. Thanks to Nairn, the word 'crisis', especially when conjoined to the phrase 'British state', is worth about as much as a Weimar deutschmark.

31   W Thompson, op cit, p320. Ironically, Anderson himself abandoned the classical Marxist perspective shortly afterwards. His own account dates this from the mid-1980s. See P Anderson, 'Foreword', *A Zone Of Engagement* (London and New York, 1992), pxii-xiii.

32   T Nairn, 'From Civil Society to Civic Nationalism', *Faces of Nationalism*, p82. The quote by Neil Harding is from 'Intellectuals, Socialism and Proletariat', in J Jennings and A Kemp-Walsh (eds), *Intellectuals And Politics* (London, 1997), p211.

33   See, for example, the remarks by H Stuart Hughes on the concept of 'hegemony': 'As happened so often in Gramsci's writings, a totalitarian thought was clothed in liberal guise.' *Consciousness And Society* (St Albans, 1974).

34   'Introduction: On Studying Nationalism', op cit, pp10-11.

35   Ibid, p13.

36   'Does Tomorrow Belong to the Bullets or the Bouquets?', *New Statesman And Society*, 19 June 1992, p31. The appropriate response to this irrationalism was given by a fellow Scottish nationalist, Pat Kane, who condemned the resort to 'biological or species-hereditary determinations': 'The only universally-binding terms which might help us through this international liberation-chaos are not our hominid instincts, but those "circumstances of Modernity" which Nairn foolishly attempts to go behind... Pursuing a progressive-nationalist game with the cards of biological science means that your opponent may defeat you, still playing poker—but with higher, more terrifying stakes, holding infinitely dirtier and dishonest hands. The packet of nationality and biology should be left unopened, in the drawer of the first half of this century.' 'Scotland by Starlight', *Tinsel Show* (Edinburgh, 1992), p198.

37   T Nairn, 'Demonising Nationality', *Faces of Nationalism*, p63.

38   T Nairn, 'The Curse of Rurality: Limits of Modernisation Theory', *Faces of Nationalism*, pp90-92, 101-102, 109-110.

39   T Nairn, 'Reflections of Nationalist Disasters', *New Left Review* 230, July/August 1998, p149.

40   Z Bauman, *Modernity and the Holocaust* (2nd edition, Oxford, 1991), pp46, 61.

41   G Eley, 'The British Model and the German Road: Rethinking the Course of German History Before 1914', in D Blackbourn and G Eley, *The Peculiarities of German History* (Oxford, 1984), p154.

42   N Stone, *Europe Transformed: 1878-1919* (Glasgow, 1983), p160.

43   Z Bauman, op cit, px.

44   T Nairn, 'The Curse of Rurality', op cit, p149.

45   T Nairn, 'Micro-States', *Faces of Nationalism*, pp143-149.

46   T Nairn, 'The Owl of Minerva', *Faces of Nationalism*, p52.

47   T Nairn, 'Demonising Nationality', op cit, pp57-58.

48   B Arnot and K Buketov, 'The Political Economy of Russian Labour: From Aquiesence to Action?', *Abertay Sociology Papers* 1:2 (University of Abertay, 1998), pp7, 9.

49   T Nairn, 'The Question of Scale', *Faces of Nationalism*, p134.

50   T Nairn, 'Internationalism: a Critique', *Faces of Nationalism*, p32.

51   Ibid, p30.

52   Ibid, p35.

53   Even this apparent recognition that internationalism once sprung unforced from a pre-lapsarian proletariat is designed to emphasise the supposed extent of the subsequent fall. In fact, even in their formative years, most proletarians have had to overcome reformist consciousness, strategy and organisation—of which nationalism is inevitably a component. I have discussed this in the context of Scotland in two forthcoming books, *Discovering The Scottish Revolution: The Decline of Scottish Feudal Society and the Origins of the British Capitalist State, 1688-1746*, Conclusion, and *Highlanders Into Scots, Scots Into Britons: The Origins of National Consciousness in Scotland, 1746-1820*, ch 8 and Conclusion.

54   Ibid, pp32-33, 36.

55   A Callinicos, *Theories And Narratives* (Cambridge, 1995), p179.

56   A D Smith, *The Ethnic Origins Of Nations*, op cit, pp11-2, 8.

57   E Gellner, *Nationalism*, op cit, pp7-8.
58   T Nairn 'Introduction: On Studying Nationalism', *Faces of Nationalism*, p7. This is a good example of one of Nairn's most annoying habits: quoting an argument against one of his positions in a knowing kind of way—then carrying on without actually answering the point.
59   T Nairn, 'Union and Empire', *Faces of Nationalism*, p209.
60   In particular, E Gellner, 'Nationalism', *Thought And Change* (London, 1964). See the references in *The Break-Up of Britain*, pp96, 99, 133, 317, 338, 342 and 358. As we saw above, his attitude to the Gellner thesis has now undergone a significant alteration.
61   N Harris, *Of Bread And Guns* (Harmondsworth, 1982), p24.
62   B Anderson, op cit, p36.
63   C Harman, op cit, pp42, 43.
64   The problem for both Anderson and Nairn may have been their incomprehension at the conflicts between supposedly socialist—or at least 'post-capitalist'—states in Indochina from 1978 onwards. Compare B Anderson, op cit, pp xi, 1-2, and T Nairn, 'Postscript 1981: Into Political Emergency', op cit, p371.
65   G Kerevan, 'The Origins of Scottish Nationhood: Arguments Within Scottish Marxism', *The Bulletin Of Scottish Politics*, 1:2, Spring 1981, p118-119.
66   Occasionally the mask slipped even prior to 1989. When Khieu Samphan, one of the leaders of the Khmer Rouge, was interviewed in January 1981, his response was rather different: 'No more socialism. No more socialist revolution... Our ideal is the survival of Cambodia. As for Communism, we saw it as the way to lead Cambodia to independence and survival—a means only, not the ideal. Now, through the flesh and blood of people, we have been given the experience to know that we cannot follow this way.' Quoted in G Evans and K Rowley, *Red Brotherhood At War* (London, 1984), p251.
67   This was true even during the First World War, which Nairn repeatedly cites as an example of spontaneous national feeling. The issue has been dealt with in recent editions of this journal, so I will not repeat the arguments here. See M Trudell, 'Prelude to Revolution: Class Consciousness and the First World War, *International Socialism* 2:76, Autumn 1997, pp71-85, supplemented by I Birchall, 'The Vice-Like Hold of Nationalism? A Comment on Megan Trudell's 'Prelude to Revolution' *International Socialism* 2:78, Spring 1978.
68   The following two paragraphs are based on information and—in the case of the first—analysis contained in A Callinicos and M Simons, *The Great Strike*: *International Socialism* 2:27/8, Spring/Summer 1985, pp84-92, and K Aitken, *The Bairns O' Adam* (Edinburgh, 1997), pp273-281. The latter is a semi-official history of the Scottish TUC.
69   Quoted in J Owens, *Miners 1984-1994* (Edinburgh, 1994), p91. The editor and the interviewee are not the same person.
70   K Aitken, op cit, p292.
71   Ibid, p295.
72   A Law, 'Neither Historic Nor Colonial': Workers' Organisation in a Scottish Dockyard', in A Day and K Lum (eds), *A History Of Labour In The Royal Dockyards* (London, forthcoming). One the stewards was Alex Falconer, who became the Labour MEP for Fife and Mid-Scotland in 1984. I am grateful to Alex Law for showing me this article prior to publication.
73   J Pilger, 'The Dockers', *Hidden Agendas* (London, 1998), p351.
74   T Nairn, 'From Civil Society to Civic Nationalism', pp87, 88, my emphasis.
75   Ibid, p84.
76   T Nairn, 'Identities in Scotland', *Faces of Nationalism*, p187.
77   Ibid, p193. This was written in March 1991.
78   R Burnett, 'Socialists and the SNP', in G Brown (ed), op cit, p121.

79   *The Scotsman*, 5 June 1998.
80   J McMillan, 'Foreign Lesson in Pressing for Home Rule', *Scotland On Sunday*, 22
      August 1993.
81   *The Scotsman*, 1 July 1998.
82   See N Davidson and K McKechnie, 'Riotous Assembly?', *Socialist Review* 219,
      May 1998, pp4-5.
83   T Nairn, 'Sovereignty After the Election', *Faces of Nationalism*, p221.
84   Ibid, p223. The reference here to 'recalling' Parliament presumably aludes to the
      feudal estates which dissolved themselves on 28 April 1707!
85   'British Sovereignty Since the Election', *Scottish Affairs*, Special Issue,
      Understanding Constitutional Change, 1998, p36. Nairn's contribution begins
      with an unseemly grovel to Donald Dewar 'our last and greatest Scottish Secretary
      of State', who had preceded him on the platform. So much for the iniquities of the
      Labour Party. See ibid, p13.
86   P Surridge, L Patterson, A Brown and D McCrone, 'The Scottish Electorate and
      the Scottish Parliament', *Understanding Constitutional Change*, p43.
87   T Nairn, 'Empire and Union', *Faces of Nationalism*, p208.
88   'Scots Awa', *The Economist*, 26 May-1 June 1990, pp18-19.
89   A Gowers, 'L'Ecosse Libre', *Financial Times*, 14 August 1998.
90   A Neil, 'Scotland the Self-Deluded', *The Spectator*, 15 August 1998, p12. I am
      unable to recall the source of this memorable piece of Nairnian invective—aimed
      at a deserving target, for once—but it springs to mind every time Neil's
      sanctimonious features loom out over one his odious op-ed pieces in *The
      Scotsman*, a paper which regularly falls, under his regime as editor-in-chief, to
      new lows of right wing hysteria.
91   T Nairn, 'Race and Nationalism', *Faces of Nationalism*, p121.
92   'Why it Happened', A Quattrochi and T Nairn, *The Beginning Of The End*
      (London, 1968), p173. A review of the reissue of this book by Jonathan Neale
      recommends that readers 'skip the second half of the book, by Tom Nairn'. '1968:
      The Year the Monolith Cracked', *Socialist Review* 219, May 1998, p17. It is true
      that in comparison with Quattrochi's Situationalist fireworks Nairn's contribution
      seems rather drab, but in comparison with the latter's other work, both before and
      since, it positively soars.
93   T Nairn, 'The Three Dreams of Scottish Nationalism', *Memoirs Of A Modern
      Scotland*, op cit, p54.
94   L D Trotsky, 'The Tragedy of the German Proletariat: the German Workers Will
      Rise Again—Stalinism, Never!', in G Breitman and M Maisel (eds), *The Struggle
      Against Fascism In Germany* (New York, 1971), p377.

The Socialist Workers Party is one of an international grouping of socialist organisations:

AUSTRALIA	International Socialists, PO Box A338, Sydney South
BRITAIN	Socialist Workers Party, PO Box 82, London E3
CANADA	International Socialists, PO Box 339, Station E, Toronto, Ontario M6H 4E3
CYPRUS	Ergatiki Demokratia, PO Box 7280, Nicosia
DENMARK	Internationale Socialister, Postboks 642, 2200 København N
GERMANY	Linksruck, Postfach 304 183, 20359 Hamburg
GREECE	Sosialistiko Ergatiko Komma, c/o Workers Solidarity, PO Box 8161, Athens 100 10
HOLLAND	Internationale Socialisten, PO Box 92052, 1090AA Amsterdam
IRELAND	Socialist Workers Party, PO Box 1648, Dublin 8
NEW ZEALAND	Socialist Workers Organization, PO Box 8851, Auckland
NORWAY	Internasjonale Socialisterr, Postboks 9226 Grønland, 0134 Oslo
POLAND	Solidarność Socjalistyczna, PO Box 12, 01-900 Warszawa 118
SPAIN	Socialismo Internacional, Apartado 563, 08080 Barcelona
UNITED STATES	International Socialist Organisation, PO Box 16085, Chicago, Illinois 60616
ZIMBABWE	International Socialist Organisation, PO Box 6758, Harare

The following issues of *International Socialism* (second series) are available price £3 (including postage) from IS Journal, PO Box 82, London E3 3LH. *International Socialism* 2:58 and 2:65 are available on cassette from the Royal National Institute for the Blind (Peterborough Library Unit). Phone 01733 370777.

International Socialism 2:81 Winter 1998
Alex Callinicos: World capitalism at the abyss ★ Mike Haynes and Pete Glatter: The Russian catastrophe ★ Phil Marfleet: Globalisation and the Third World ★ Lindsey German: In a class of its own ★ Judy Cox: John Reed: reporting on the revolution ★ Kevin Ovenden: The resistible rise of Adolf Hitler ★

International Socialism 2:80 Autumn 1998
Clare Fermont: Indonesia: the inferno of revolution ★ Workers' representatives and socialists: Three interviews from Indonesia ★ Chris Bambery: Report from Indonesia ★ Tony Cliff: Revolution and counter-revolution: lessons for Indonesia ★ John Molyneux: The legitimacy of modern art ★ Gary McFarlane: A respectable trade? Slavery and the rise of capitalism ★ Paul McGarr: The French Revolution: Marxism versus capitalism ★ Shaun Doherty: Will the real James Connolly please stand up? ★

International Socialism 2:79 Summer 1998
John Rees: The return of Marx? ★ Lindsey German: Reflections on *The Communist Manifesto* ★ Judy Cox: An introduction to Marx's theory of alienation ★ Judith Orr: Making a comeback: the Marxist theory of crisis ★ Megan Trudell: New Labour, old conflicts: the story so far ★ John Molyneux: State of the art ★ Anna Chen: In perspective: Sergei Eisenstein ★ Jonathan Neale: Vietnam Veterans ★ Phil Gasper: Bookwatch: Marxism and science ★

International Socialism 2:78 Spring 1998
Colin Sparks: The eye of the storm ★ Shin Gyoung-hee: The crisis and the workers' movement in South Korea ★ Rob Hoveman: Financial crises and the real economy ★ Peter Morgan: Class divisions in the gay community ★ Alex Callinicos: The secret of the dialectic ★ John Parrington: It's life, Jim, but not as we know it ★ Judy Cox: Robin Hood: earl, outlaw or rebel? ★ Ian Birchall: The vice-like hold of nationalism? A comment on Megan Trudell's 'Prelude to revolution' ★ William Keach: In perspective: Alexander Cockburn and Christopher Hitchens ★

International Socialism 2:77 Winter 1997
Audrey Farrell: Addicted to profit—capitalism and drugs ★ Mike Gonzalez: The resurrections of Che Guevara ★ Sam Ashman: India: imperialism, partition and resistance ★ Henry Maitles: Never Again! ★ John Baxter: The return of political science ★ Dave Renton: Past its peak ★

International Socialism 2:76 Autumn 1997
Mike Haynes: Was there a parliamentary alternative in 1917? ★ Megan Trudell: Prelude to revolution: class consciousness and the First World War ★ Judy Cox: A light in the darkness ★ Pete Glatter: Victor Serge: writing for the future ★ Gill Hubbard: A guide to action ★ Chris Bambery: Review article: Labour's history of hope and despair ★

International Socialism 2:75 Summer 1997
John Rees: The class struggle under New Labour ★ Alex Callinicos: Europe: the mounting crisis ★ Lance Selfa: Mexico after the Zapatista uprising ★ William Keach: Rise like lions? Shelley and the revolutionary left ★ Judy Cox: What state are we really in? ★ John Parrington: In perspective: Valentin Voloshinov ★

International Socialism 2:74 Spring 1997
Colin Sparks: Tories, Labour and the crisis in education ★ Colin Wilson: The politics of information technology ★ Mike Gonzalez: No more heroes: Nicaragua 1996 ★ Christopher Hill: Tulmults and commotions: turning the world upside down ★ Peter Morgan: Capitalism without frontiers? ★ Alex Callinicos: Minds, machines and evolution ★ Anthony Arnove: In perspective: Noam Chomsky★

International Socialism 2:73 Winter 1996
Chris Harman: Globalisation: a critique of a new orthodoxy ★ Chris Bambery: Marxism and sport ★ John Parrington: Computers and consciousness: a reply to Alex Callinicos ★ Joe Faith: Dennett, materialism and empiricism ★ Megan Trudell: Who made the American Revolution? ★ Mark O'Brien: The class conflicts which shaped British history ★ John Newsinger: From class war to Cold War ★ Alex Callinicos: The state in debate ★ Charlie Kimber: Review article: coming to terms with barbarism in Rwanda in Burundi★

International Socialism 2:72 Autumn 1996
Alex Callinicos: Betrayal and discontent: Labour under Blair ★ Sue Cockerill and Colin Sparks: Japan in crisis ★ Richard Levins: When science fails us ★ Ian Birchall: The Babeuf bicentenary: conspiracy or revolutionary party? ★ Brian Manning: A voice for the poor ★ Paul O'Flinn: From the kingdom of necessity to the kingdom of freedom: Morris's *News from Nowhere* ★ Clare Fermont: Bookwatch: Palestine and the Middle East 'peace process'★

International Socialism 2:71 Summer 1996
Chris Harman: The crisis of bourgeois economics ★ Hassan Mahamdallie: William Morris and revolutionary Marxism ★ Alex Callinicos: Darwin, materialism and revolution ★ Chris Nineham: Raymond Williams: revitalising the left? ★ Paul Foot: A passionate prophet of liberation ★ Gill Hubbard: Why has feminism failed women? ★ Lee Sustar: Bookwatch: fighting to unite black and white★

International Socialism 2:70 Spring 1996
Alex Callinicos: South Africa after apartheid ★ Chris Harman: France's hot December ★ Brian Richardson: The making of a revolutionary ★ Gareth Jenkins: Why Lucky Jim turned right—an obituary of Kingsley Amis ★ Mark O'Brien: The bloody birth of capitalism ★ Lee Humber: Studies in revolution ★ Adrian Budd: A new life for Lenin ★ Martin Smith: Bookwatch: the General Strike★

International Socialism 2:69 Winter 1995
Lindsey German: The Balkan war: can there be peace? ★ Duncan Blackie: The left and the Balkan war ★ Nicolai Gentchev: The myth of welfare dependency ★ Judy Cox: Wealth, poverty and class in Britain today ★ Peter Morgan: Trade unions and strikes ★ Julie Waterson: The party at its peak ★ Megan Trudell: Living to some purpose ★ Nick Howard: The rise and fall of socialism in one city ★ Andy Durgan: Bookwatch: Civil war and revolution in Spain ★

International Socialism 2:68 Autumn 1995
Ruth Brown: Racism and immigration in Britain ★ John Molyneux: Is Marxism deterministic? ★ Stuart Hood: News from nowhere? ★ Lee Sustar: Communism in the heart of the beast ★ Peter Linebaugh: To the teeth and forehead of our faults ★ George Paizis: Back to the future ★ Phil Marshall: The children of stalinism ★ Paul D'Amato: Bookwatch: 100 years of cinema ★

International Socialism 2:67 Summer 1995
Paul Foot: When will the Blair bubble burst? ★ Chris Harman: From Bernstein to Blair—100 years of revisionism ★ Chris Bambery: Was the Second World War a war for democracy? ★ Alex Callinicos: Hope against the Holocaust ★Chris Nineham: Is the media all powerful? ★ Peter Morgan: How the West was won ★ Charlie Hore: Bookwatch: China since Mao ★

International Socialism 2:66 Spring 1995
Dave Crouch: The crisis in Russia and the rise of the right ★ Phil Gasper: Cruel and unusual punishment: the politics of crime in the United States ★ Alex Callinicos: Backwards to liberalism ★ John Newsinger: Matewan: film and working class struggle ★ John Rees: The light and the dark ★ Judy Cox: How to make the Tories disappear ★ Charlie Hore: Jazz: a reply to the critics ★ Pat Riordan: Bookwatch: Ireland ★

International Socialism 2:65 Special issue
Lindsey German: Frederick Engels: life of a revolutionary ★ John Rees: Engels' Marxism ★ Chris Harman: Engels and the origins of human society ★ Paul McGarr: Engels and natural science ★

International Socialism 2:63 Summer 1994
Alex Callinicos: Crisis and class struggle in Europe today ★ Duncan Blackie: The United Nations and the politics of imperialism ★ Brian Manning: The English Revolution and the transition from feudalism to capitalism ★ Lee Sustar: The roots of multi-racial labour unity in the United States ★ Peter Linebaugh: Days of villainy: a reply to two critics ★ Dave Sherry: Trotsky's last, greatest struggle ★ Peter Morgan: Geronimo and the end of the Indian wars ★ Dave Beecham: Ignazio Silone and *Fontamara* ★ Chris Bambery: Bookwatch: understanding fascism ★

International Socialism 2:62 Spring 1994
Sharon Smith: Mistaken identity—or can identity politics liberate the oppressed? ★ Iain Ferguson: Containing the crisis—crime and the Tories ★ John Newsinger: Orwell and the Spanish Revolution ★ Chris Harman: Change at the first millenium ★ Adrian Budd: Nation and empire—Labour's foreign policy 1945-51 ★ Gareth Jenkins: Novel questions ★ Judy Cox: Blake's revolution ★ Derek Howl: Bookwatch: the Russian Revolution ★

International Socialism 2:39 Summer 1988
Chris Harman and Andy Zebrowski: Glasnost, before the storm ★ Chanie Rosenberg: Labour and the fight against fascism ★ Mike Gonzalez: Central America after the Peace Plan ★ Ian Birchall: Raymond Williams ★ Alex Callinicos: Reply to John Rees ★

International Socialism 2:35 Summer 1987
Pete Green: Capitalism and the Thatcher years ★ Alex Callinicos: Imperialism, capitalism and the state today ★ Ian Birchall: Five years of *New Socialist* ★ Callinicos and Wood debate 'Looking for alternatives to reformism' ★ David Widgery replies on 'Beating Time' ★

International Socialism 2:30 Autumn 1985
Gareth Jenkins: Where is the Labour Party heading? ★ David McNally: Debt, inflation and the rate of profit ★ Ian Birchall: The terminal crisis in the British Communist Party ★ replies on Women's oppression and *Marxism Today* ★

International Socialism 2:26 Spring 1985
Pete Green: Contradictions of the American boom ★ Colin Sparks: Labour and imperialism ★ Chris Bambery: Marx and Engels and the unions ★ Sue Cockerill: The municipal road to socialism ★ Norah Carlin: Is the family part of the superstructure? ★ Kieran Allen: James Connolly and the 1916 rebellion ★

International Socialism 2:25 Autumn 1984
John Newsinger: Jim Larkin, Syndicalism and the 1913 Dublin Lockout ★ Pete Binns: Revolution and state capitalism in the Third World ★ Colin Sparks: Towards a police state? ★ Dave Lyddon: Demystifying the downturn ★ John Molyneux: Do working class men benefit from women's oppression? ★

International Socialism 2:18 Winter 1983
Donny Gluckstein: Workers' councils in Western Europe ★ Jane Ure Smith: The early Communist press in Britain ★ John Newsinger: The Bolivian Revolution ★ Andy Durgan: Largo Caballero and Spanish socialism ★ M Barker and A Beezer: Scarman and the language of racism ★

International Socialism 2:14 Winter 1981
Chris Harman: The riots of 1981 ★ Dave Beecham: Class struggle under the Tories ★ Tony Cliff: Alexandra Kollontai ★ L James and A Paczuska: Socialism needs feminism ★ reply to Cliff on Zetkin ★ Feminists In the labour movement ★

International Socialism 2:13 Summer 1981
Chris Harman: The crisis last time ★ Tony Cliff: Clara Zetkin ★ Ian Birchall: Left Social Democracy In the French Popular Front ★ Pete Green: Alternative Economic Strategy ★ Tim Potter: The death of Eurocommunism ★